"THIS TENDER VINE"

"THIS TENDER VINE"

HOLDERNESS SCHOOL AT 125 YEARS

Judith B. Solberg

iUniverse, Inc.
New York Lincoln Shanghai

"THIS TENDER VINE"
HOLDERNESS SCHOOL AT 125 YEARS

iUniverse books may be ordered through booksellers or by contacting:

iUniverse
2021 Pine Lake Road, Suite 100
Lincoln, NE 68512
www.iuniverse.com
1-800-Authors (1-800-288-4677)

ISBN: 0-595-33966-2 (pbk)
ISBN: 0-595-67043-1 (cloth)

Printed in the United States of America

Contents

Foreword

As Head of Holderness School during our 125th year celebration, I was fortunate to have a front-row seat during an exciting year of reflection. Both this work and Judith Solberg's other book, *Holderness School: 125 Years in Pictures*, are symbols not only of the year, but of the unbelievably rich history that has resulted in Holderness School being the exceptional place that it is today. The School's history is full of riveting drama and larger-than-life folks who believed in this small school with its unique mission.

For me it has been both humbling and inspiring to read these tales and, through them, meet the people who are the history of Holderness School. I am confident that you too will find the tales inspiring.

On behalf of the Holderness School community, I would like to extend our appreciation to the Holderness School historians upon whose work Judith Solberg has so ably built this book. The 75-year history was a thoughtful and insightful work of love written by Edric Weld the year after he stepped down as Headmaster. Twenty-five years later a graceful appendix and update was added to that work by Pat Henderson. Work for *"This Tender Vine"* began with the caring and diligent work of archivist Rachel Saliba. When Rachel left, we were blessed that Judith Solberg became our archivist and the author of this important synthesis of Holderness School's stories.

Phil Peck
November, 2004

Preface

I was truly lucky to have the opportunity to come to Holderness School and undertake the writing of this school history. When the administration first approached me about the project on the threshold of the school's 125th anniversary year, I began the task new to the school's culture and history. I was soon completely immersed in the personalities and events of the school's past, and though I suppose I originally offered an outsider's perspective, any distance I felt quickly evolved into affection for this remarkable little school by the lakes and mountains.

The organization of this book is first meant to provide a chronological overview of important school events, and then to delve more deeply into thematic areas that are core to the school. I have used the headmasters' tenures as convenient time markers, but it is not my intention to imply that the headmasters alone influenced the school's history. Students, parents, alumni, trustees, faculty and staff members—all these groups of exceptional people have shaped the course of the school. However, as much as possible, I have chosen to focus on the institution rather than on individuals. I have attempted to strike a fair balance, noting individuals whose innovations helped to mold the school's identity, without listing all of the outstanding personal contributions made over the years. Indeed, if I had tried to do so, the book would be three times its length, and I surely would never have reached the events of the present day.

For similar reasons, I have relied primarily upon the holdings of the Holderness School Archives rather than on personal interviews or outside research. I have been lucky enough to meet and talk with a few notable members of the extended Holderness School family, and whenever possible, I have used those perspectives to inform this book. There are many more individuals whose stories and experiences can enrich the history presented here, and this book is by no means representative of all of the valuable observations that such an undertaking might yield.

Instead, my goal was to draw a picture of the school that was principally based on reference materials held by the school. These materials have included photographs, yearbooks, written histories, personal reflections, school newspapers and magazines, the lectures and correspondence of past headmasters, flyers from concerts and plays, school catalogs, and a variety of other materials. There is an enormous amount of information to be found in the archives, and it will provide a rich resource for interested members of the school community for the foreseeable future.

Inasmuch as our school records are incomplete, however, this book is also necessarily limited in scope and is only as accurate as its source material allows. I take comfort in the fact that our understanding of history is never complete. Rather, history is a patchwork quilt whose colors and patterns change as we add to our knowledge—one small fact can influence the entire impression that we have of a particular subject. I can say without hesitation that, by the next anniversary year, the school will be in a position to greatly add to what I have presented here.

Acknowledgements

As any student of history knows, we are all dependent on the stories others have told before us. I relied heavily on previous school histories as I embarked on this project, and it would have been impossible to grasp the framework of the school's past without the work of numerous other authors. Anniversary histories of the school written by William Porter Niles (fifty years), Edric Weld (seventy-five years), and Pat Henderson (one hundred years) were particularly helpful. For early Holderness history, two works by George Hodges were essential; I heartily recommend them to anyone who also has an interest in the early days of the Episcopal Church in New Hampshire. A multitude of (often anonymous) student authors in school publications helped paint a picture of residential life, and led me—I hope—toward a more accurate representation of what life was like at Holderness School during each era.

The images reproduced with this text are all held in the school's archives. Although most photographs in these archives are unattributed, a few that appear here can be credited. These include the photos of Rev. Balch (William Notman), Don Henderson's trail crew (Robert Bull), students gathering wood for the Bioshelter (Bob Terhune), the school production of H.M.S. Pinafore (Avery Rogers), and the portrait of Phil Peck (Linda Himmer). I am very grateful for the glass slides given to the school by George Clark of the class of 1895; they provide many of the key images we have of early school life. Finally, I would like to acknowledge the work of the late Herbert Waters, who taught at Holderness School for many years. He created the beautiful woodcut that appears on the front cover, showing a view of campus from inside Livermore Hall.

I also wish to recognize the many people who have given time and energy toward the completion of this book. To begin with, Rachel Saliba grounded me in the basics of the Holderness School Archives, and set me up for success from the start. The entire Alumni and Development team, and Christine Louis and Peg Hendel in particular, supported my efforts and provided context when I needed it. Rick Carey, Phil Peck, Jessica Juliuson, Pat Henderson, Pete Woodward and others were willing readers and suggestion-providers throughout the process. All of the faculty shared information and expressed interest in the project—and many of them also endured my trivia-spouting during lunch.

Members of the extended Holderness School family have been extremely generous with their time and reflections. Numerous alumni and former faculty have shared their memories of days past via the school's website, helping to bring the history alive for me and for current students. Pete Woodward, Rip Richards, Jim Brewer, Pat and Don Henderson, Dave Lockwood, Janice Pedrin-Nielson and others have spent time speaking with me personally, developing my understanding of particular areas. Mary Anne (Weld) Bodecker merits special thanks for sharing memories of her childhood, and for helping to bring back other family members and alumni with more to say.

Finally, current Head of School Phil Peck has been unfailingly positive and supportive of this project since its inception over a year ago. I have greatly appreciated both the guidance he provided about structure and direction, and the freedom of pace and perspective that he has afforded me. It has been a privilege to rediscover lost history with him.

Introduction

Those who have been a part of the Holderness School community equate the institution with long-held traditions and a venerable history. They are not wrong. Students today attend services in the same chapel as their predecessors; the school still owes much of its character to breathtaking New Hampshire surroundings; the residential experience continues to reflect the close bonds of family life.

Continuity is not the only story to be told of Holderness School, however. The school's history is filled with quiet triumphs over fierce challenges. Indeed, the ability to overcome such challenges may be the defining characteristic of the school. Again and again, Holderness School has risen like a phoenix from fire—sometimes literally—and defied expectations to become a stronger and better place.

The challenges that faced the school were, at times, daunting. Although Holderness School's founders were committed to avoiding debt, unexpected events combined to make this hope unsustainable. An 1882 fire burned the school to the ground, forcing the trustees to refund tuition and rebuild; despite many generous contributions, the trustees had to assume debt in order to continue.[1] This step began a cycle of financial strain that haunted the school during the first seventy-five years of its history.

Fiscal struggles magnified other challenges, and sometimes were their root cause. The need for low salaries led to high faculty turnover, making it difficult for the young school to develop its academic reputation. An austere physical plant deterred a number of prospective students, resulting in some periods of low enrollment. Perhaps the most damaging effect of debt management, however, was that the school had few financial reserves with which to face unexpected crises. War-time restrictions, a second devastating campus fire, the Depression—all of these ordeals awaited the school.

At times, the difficulties seemed too great to overcome. After the 1931 fire, the board accepted the resignations of several trustees who disagreed with the decision to rebuild the school.[2] When the headmastership of Edric Weld ended in 1951, the board still faced many challenges. As one member recalled:

1

Times were not easy for a small school, lacking endowment, and far in the north country without benefit of the interstates we now take for granted. On several occasions, the trustees debated vigorously whether the School should close.[3]

The trustees did not close the school. Instead, they made bold strategic decisions to increase enrollment and to seek a significant endowment for the school. The resolve shown by these remarkable individuals led to a new, more stable era for the school, and assured that the institution would be able to continue into the next century.

Perseverance is a hallmark of Holderness School. The sermon given in 1879 on the school's opening day warned that "[s]uccess is not a noble start, or a loud flourish of silvery new-moon trumpets. Success is this: *fruitful continuance*."[4] Perhaps this admonition foreshadowed some of the challenges that lay ahead, cautioning students and teachers against premature complacency and self-congratulation. But it also provided a hopeful message. Whether thriving or discouraged, the school's success would be measured by how it faced its future.

To have faith in the future required faith in a greater power—as the sermon pointed out, only God could assure the success of any endeavor. It closed by invoking a blessing from this higher power, and by requesting protection in the days and years to come:

> Plant Thou this tender vine. Prepare Thou room, abundant room, and good, before it. Cause it to take deep root; to hang with gladdening clusters. Amid our hills let it branch out with boughs like goodly cedars. Let it send them to the sea; its branches to the river. Look down from heaven on us. Behold this vine. Be it a vine Thy hand hath planted. Let no one break its hedges down, that all who pass may pluck it. Let not the heedless hand destroy, nor malice devour and ravage. Let not the fire or axe come near it. But turn, O Lord of Hosts, and cause thy face to shine upon it. Amen.[5]

The school was to face its share of literal and figurative fires. However, the community approached such challenges with courage, and Holderness School emerged stronger from each trial. Exceptional people with exceptional determination and faith have shepherded the school through troubled times, and fortified the foundations of the institution along the way. The stories that remain with us, therefore, are those of development and improvement, of continuity and triumph. These are the stories upon which this history will linger. For after all, as the school moved through its history, the "tender vine" did indeed take root, and flourish.

Foundations

A TOWN IS BORN

The town where the Holderness School is located holds the distinction of having been created twice. The first charter for Holderness was granted in 1751 by Benning Wentworth, the first Royal Governor of New Hampshire. The namesake for the town is Robert D'Arcy, who was the Secretary of State at the time that the charter was granted. D'Arcy was the fourth and last Earl of Holderness, a peninsula in Yorkshire, England. Some have found it amusing that "this very up and down area [was named] after a piece of flat seacoast."[6]

Though not a resident, the Earl of Holderness did show an interest in this new area of settlement. Indian raiders who were headed to Canada frequently took settlers captive at that time, so it was "a very much suspected area as far as safety went."[7] At one point in 1754, D'Arcy advised the Governors of the Colonies to "form a Union for mutual protection and defense against the combined French and Indians"—which advice may have planted the seed that led to the eventual formation of the United States.[8] Peace did not come until 1758, when the French were defeated in Quebec. Soon after, in 1761, the town charter was renewed under the name "New Holderness."

At this time, several interested parties drew lots for a parcel of land in Holderness. This number included a judge named Samuel Livermore. He was also in his lifetime to be a representative and senator; he is most fondly remembered for his influence on New Hampshire's decision to sign the United States Constitution. Around 1770, Livermore bought another 800 acres of Holderness land from the son of Governor Wentworth. By 1775, he had moved to Holderness (via Portsmouth and Londonderry)[9], and around 1780 he built the mansion that would, some one hundred years later, become the first home of the Holderness School for Boys.[10]

STEWARDS OF THE LAND

In the century that passed before the school began, the Livermore estate had several owners. Many of these title-holders left their marks on the land and community in ways that resonate even in current student life at Holderness School. However, the beauty and character of the land and its environs were constant, and are perhaps the greatest legacy to survive from the earliest days of the town.

The Livermore estate changed hands several times within the family itself. Samuel Livermore left it to his son Edward St. Loe Livermore in 1803, but Edward's younger brother Arthur "bought the estate from Edward at a very high price, and lived there for the next twenty-five years."[11] Arthur apparently also loved nearby Little's Falls, named for Moses Little. While living on the Livermore estate, Arthur bought the falls and some neighboring mill buildings from Moses Little's son James. It was at this point that the falls became known by their current name, Livermore Falls.[12] Eventually, Arthur purchased James Little's own home, moving into the house near the falls and selling the Livermore estate.[13]

James Joy, a "successful farmer from Pittsfield, N.H.," is believed to have bought the Livermore estate in 1827, and the Joy family retained ownership until about 1850.[14] During this time, the bluff upon which the school now stands became known as Joy Hill. Edric Weld later noted with some amusement that the name "typified the feeling of the boys who rejoiced in all that surrounded the school buildings, if not in their studies."[15] The Joy family eventually sold a significant portion of the estate to James M. Whiton.[16]

The Whiton family came to Plymouth and Holderness around 1850, which was an exciting time: the first train pulled into Plymouth in that year, and James Whiton was intimately involved with the Boston, Concord, and Montreal Railroad.[17] In their short time as stewards of the Livermore estate, the Whiton family had a lasting impact. They did not live in the Livermore Mansion, but in a temporary home that was referred to as "The Lodge" located across the street from where the school's Chapel of the Holy Cross currently stands. It replaced a "white farm building" and was "a charming English-type cottage, painted red with diamond paned windows, and low ceilings."[18] The family lived there for several years until "a large brick gabled mansion" was completed nearby in 1854. This permanent home was called "Woodlands," but many also referred to it as "The House of the Seven Gables," after the Hawthorne novel.[19] From both The Lodge and Woodlands, the Whitons were able to enjoy the apples from nodhead trees they had planted.[20] These trees are still producing fruit near the school's South Campus dormitories.

Sadly, Whiton died unexpectedly in 1857, leaving a young family behind. Upon his early death, Squire Leverett (a Plymouth lawyer) took charge of the sale of the estate. According to an 1891 school account, "the most productive farming land this side of Boston" now "began to run down, and after passing through many hands was purchased by Dean Balch."[21]

Rev. Lewis P. W. Balch, Jr., circa 1867

Rev. Lewis Penn Witherspoon Balch Jr., former Dean of the Cathedral of Toronto, moved into Woodlands with his wife Emily and their family in the early 1860s.[22] Balch became the rector at nearby Trinity Church, which had fallen into disuse since the death of its first pastor, Rev. Robert Fowle, in 1847.[23] Balch had a strong interest in education and hoped to start a school; sadly, he died before doing so. His family hoped to fulfill his dream of starting a school, but was unsure how to go about doing so. In the end, it was another man's vision that set things in motion.

ENVISIONING A SCHOOL

In 1870 New Hampshire's second bishop, the Right Reverend William Woodruff Niles, was elected.[24] A former professor of Latin at Trinity College, Bishop Niles "looked forward to the time when he might found a school or schools in the diocese." Just four years after Bishop Niles was elected, the Episcopal General Convention resolved to create a Standing Committee on Education.[25]

William Woodruff Niles, circa 1860

The 1875 Committee was composed of clerical and lay leaders who were strongly committed to education in the state. Several of these committee members had ties to St. Paul's School, another New Hampshire Episcopal school that had been founded in 1856. The most notable of these members were Rev. Henry A. Coit (the first Rector of St. Paul's School) and Rev. Henry Ferguson (who would become the third Rector of St. Paul's School).[26] The committee quickly resolved to plan a church school "whose great object shall be to combine the highest degree of excellence in instruction and care-taking with the lowest possible charge for tuition and board."[27] Bishop Niles also felt that, though schools like St. Paul's were drawing students from around the country, the "community in which his lot had been cast needed also schools of high grade for the boys and girls who had been born and might be expected to spend their lives in it."[28] The school needed to be both financially accessible and of high quality.

In 1876, the committee chose a board of trustees for the planned school; these men were charged with obtaining facilities for the school, and opening it to students in 1878. Bishop Niles underscored that "[i]f the vital thing is to be gained, namely, an inexpensive school, there should be no heavy debt incurred at the outset."[29] Possible facilities were offered in the towns of Drewsville and Charlestown, but another offer included land and buildings located on the Livermore estate. This last proposal was tendered by Emily Balch, who had seen an opportunity to make her late husband's dream become reality, through her agent. It should be noted that Mrs. Balch's agent, Henry W. Blair, was well-known in the nearby town of Plymouth. A former teacher and soon-to-be U.S. Senator, Blair had also encouraged the establishment of the Plymouth Normal School in 1870, and had purchased, moved, and renovated Plymouth's old Daniel Webster Courthouse before donating it to the Young Ladies Library Association.[30]

The offer from Emily Balch was too inviting to pass up, and in September of 1878, the trustees decided to locate the school on the Livermore estate. They agreed to pay $4,000 for the former Livermore Mansion and "a house which stood where the chapel now stands," fifteen acres of land surrounding the two buildings, and 100 acres of woodland from another area of the Balch estate.[31] In actual fact, the entirety of this initial cost appears to have been covered by two donors. Blair donated $3,000 of his own money; the estate of J.E. Lyon (second president of the Concord, Boston and Montreal Railroad and builder of the Pemigewasset House) donated another $1,000.[32] Though the trustees did take on a debt of $2,600 in order to obtain water rights, the Balch offer was clearly both generous and providential.[33]

The property secured, it soon became clear that renovations would be necessary before school could begin, and that involved additional costs. The trustees decided to delay opening the school for one more year in order to address the issue. Reporting to the diocese in 1878, they said:

> If the Diocese asks, why is not the school opened and the work carried on? We answer: Because we need at least $2,000 to complete our repairs, furnish the

house plainly and pay for the property. We would be honest and we wait. Help us to begin the work righteously.[34]

The trustees found the help they needed, and the Holderness School for Boys opened to students on September 11, 1879. A later poem celebrated this realization of Balch's dream, noting: "He sowed the seed with anxious care/It has sprung up, much fruit to bear."[35]

Holderness School Headmasters 1879-2001

Rev. Frederick M. Gray (1879-1886)

Rev. Frank C. Coolbaugh (1886-1892)

Rev. Lorin Webster (1892-1922)

Rev. R. Eliot Marshall (1922-1928)

Rev. Alban Richey (1929-1931)

Rev. Edric A. Weld (1931-1951)

Donald C. Hagerman (1951-1977)

Rev. Brinton W. Woodward (1977-2001)

A Tradition of Leadership

1879–1886: REV. FREDERICK M. GRAY

The first headmaster of Holderness School, Rev. Frederick M. Gray, accepted the position in part to escape the malaria in his Staten Island parish, and in part to meet a tempting challenge. As his daughter, Mrs. Eleanor Stetson, later wrote, Gray was "something of a pioneer and, loving the country, [Holderness School] appealed to him."[36] He began the adventure with the help of a single teaching assistant, Mr. Charles H. Hough.[37]

Appropriately enough, the first student enrolled at the school was a son of the Balch family, Stephen Elliott Balch.[38] He came as a young preparatory student, and remained for nine years, continuing his studies through 1888.[39] Balch was one of fifteen boarding students and "a dozen or so day scholars" who attended during the school's first year.[40] Though the school had been conceived as a way of "meeting the [educational] requirements and means of the clergy of the diocese," the core of the student body was drawn from military families acquainted with the headmaster.[41] Apparently these boys had to take some early challenges in stride:

> On account of a strike in Hartford, Conn., the beds for the dormitories did not arrive on time, so the boys had to sleep on mattresses laid on the floor. This was not a great hardship in the warm days of September, and the beds soon arrived. Things were shortly got to running in proper order.[42]

There were other adjustments to make, as well. Some students suffered from homesickness, and found Livermore Mansion gloomy in the chilly New England autumn. In the school's first month, Clyde Fitch (a classmate of Balch's who went on to be an acclaimed playwright) wrote to his mother that "the house was cold and damp," "there wasn't a solitary thing to do," and "lots of boys complain about the food."[43] His later letters reflect a happier outlook, but judging by his lively descriptions of typical Holderness School fare, the food did not improve:

We have awful fun at the table, for there is the wittiest and the funniest boy in school sitting at our end; and we always find loads of flies and things in our eatables, and he always makes remarks. To-day flies had just begun to appear, 'to be unearthed from their graves', when a long piece of dirty cord was found hanging to my fork from my potatoes, and at the same time Wood, who sits next to me, with a short struggle, extricated from a piece of pumpkin pie three lovely flies, victims of the cook; these are not all, but the rest are too numerous to mention; this on a smaller scale occurs daily.[44]

Despite the new school's growing pains, accounts of the early days under headmaster Gray impart a sense of high spirit and adventure. Perhaps this was an outgrowth of Gray's philosophy that boys behave best when you trust them to do so. There was only one written rule: boys could not use profanity, tobacco, or liquor. The school stated the simple policy that "Boys who persistently violate this rule or are known to be otherwise vicious or corrupt, will not be permitted to remain."[45]

Of course, the faculty also wisely channeled the boys' excess energy into exploration of the great outdoors—a major attraction for prospective students. If the water was deemed warm enough by the Rector, supervised boys could swim in the Pemigewasset River. Mrs. Stetson tells us of another outdoor pastime:

[My] father, through the consent of neighboring farmers, encouraged the boys to build little camps in nearby woods rather than have them go to Plymouth a mile away [...]. On Saturday afternoons they had lunch there frequently [and] cooked flap-jacks, often inviting my father.[46]

Long winters were filled with "sugaring off" parties, snowball fights, and sledding down the slope to the intervale. When warm weather reappeared, boys often took walks or went May flowering. One such outing is recorded in an 1883 student journal:

Hubbard came in and woke me at five and I went and woke Slason and we went May flowering. We got quite a number and got back about quarter past seven. After breakfast I cut them and put them in a box and sent them to Mother.[47]

Students also made outings to town, Squam Lake, or Livermore Falls, where "the view from the bridge over the falls [was] grand—the logs coming over and the river men running over the logs."[48]

Bridge over Livermore Falls, circa 1895

As advertised, Holderness School was indeed "a healthful and happy home."[49] Enrollment at the young school was on the increase, and more teachers were needed. The enormous amount of work facing the masters of the growing school must have made staffing difficult. The task at first fell on the shoulders of the Bishop, who had "full control in securing teachers" for several years.[50] In December of 1883, however, the trustees voted to give the headmaster full hiring power.[51] Gray's strategy was to market Holderness School teaching positions to young college graduates "as a step to something more."[52]

The prospect of school growth quickly affected plans for the school's physical plant. Livermore Mansion had been a tight fit for students and faculty from the beginning, and in the summer after the school's first year, the trustees "enlarged and remodeled [the building] to make accommodations for the ever-increasing number of boys."[53] Sadly, the investment in the expanded school building was to be short-lived. The historic old mansion burned in the spring of 1882, and "all the inmates, numbering about seventy persons, were rendered homeless for the time being."[54] Mrs. Stetson provides a rare glimpse of that event:

> "On one windy March afternoon, with five feet of snow in the ground, while my father was conducting a laboratory experiment, one of the work men on the place ran over to the schoolhouse, saying that the roof was on fire. Father

had always feared a defective chimney in the addition [...]. Fortunately the fire occurred in the afternoon at study-hour: all the boys could be accounted for. My father assembled the Masters, assigned each to a dormitory, had the boys tumble their belongings into trunks and slide them downstairs and out into the orchard, now the athletic ground. No boy lost anything. It is said of Billy Niles, the Bishop's son, that he grabbed his toothbrush and Bible, and rushed for the orchard! My father began saving school property. Somebody called, 'the timbers are falling.' Covered with wood-soot, my father jumped from a window. In one hour the well-seasoned old house had burned and the chimneys had fallen. By night-fall, every boy was housed in Plymouth."[55]

These generous neighbors took care of Holderness School students until trustees could send word of the school's plan. In the end, they decided to close the school until the campus could be rebuilt.[56] This decision must have involved heartache for the fledgling school's trustees, trustees who were committed to avoiding debt and maintaining affordable tuition. That September, it was deemed necessary to borrow $7,500 to cover building and maintenance expenses, and the debt increased in the ensuing months.[57] However, the trustees held firm on tuition levels, which would not budge for another six years.[58]

While the school underwent reconstruction, the boys left early for home. Some—like Fitch—would not return, choosing instead to go on to college or another school.[59] Others would return to a new, practically unrecognizable, campus:

> Plans were immediately drawn up for a large three-story, fireproof, brick building, with hollow walls and slate and metal roofs, and having accommodations for sixty boys, the Rector, his family, the masters, and all other members of the household. We are told that this building, which was called Knowlton Hall, was put up in eight weeks time. A large one-story frame building was erected for a schoolhouse. The buildings were ready for use by the fall of the same year.[60]

Life at Holderness School resumed, with some believing that the fire, "at first thought to be a great misfortune," had actually "turned out to be a blessing in disguise."[61] On the fire's anniversary, students built a bonfire in front of Knowlton Hall and "did a good deal of hollering" to celebrate.[62]

Within another year fifty-two boys were enrolled at the rebuilt school, living in gothic Knowlton Hall and pursuing studies in the Schoolhouse.[63] The campus expanded still further when a Miss Zabriskie, a New York friend of Bishop Niles, funded the construction of a new school chapel in the summer of 1884.[64] The school had previously held its religious services in old Trinity Church, but the new Chapel of the Holy Cross offered increased seating capacity. Services and daily prayers were now held in the chapel "whenever the weather permitted, and Trinity was used no more except for funeral services."[65]

Despite the turmoil and changes that faced the school during its first years, a vibrant school culture had taken root. Boys put on impromptu singing parties and dances in the dormitory, and engaged in night-time pranks when they could get away with it:

> Did not have any study hour this evening as the gas would not burn. We had a lot of fun round the house in the dark. Some hit [faculty member] Mr. Cummings with a clothes bag and like to broke his neck.[66]

Clyde Fitch wrote the school's first paper, the Thunderbolt, which others described as "full of interest and imagination."[67] Games of tennis, baseball, euchre, or marbles were common pastimes, and students learned gymnastic skills in the Old Gym.[68] High spirits remained irrepressible.

With his pioneering education project well-established, Gray decided to retire as headmaster of Holderness School in 1886. However, he retained his interest in the school and continued on the board until 1890. When he resigned this position, the remaining trustees wrote him a letter to "assure him of the excellence of his work while Rector of the School, and [of] the Board's appreciation of his labors."[69] In six short years, Gray's school had faced growing pains and unforeseen challenges, but had survived and even flourished. Not for the last time, Holderness School had risen strong from the flames.

1886–1892: REV. FRANK C. COOLBAUGH

When Frederick Gray moved on to a new position at St. Agnes's School in Albany, the Rev. Frank C. Coolbaugh became the second Rector of Holderness School.[70] Coolbaugh came to the school from pastoral work in Michigan, a graduate of Hobart who had been ordained as a deacon and a priest in 1870.[71] He was remembered by one former student as "a portly man with high color, who always wore a frock coat. He was a fine preacher and his sermons something to remember."[72] These sentiments were echoed by another student, who described Coolbaugh as "a man of warm friendly nature and a good preacher."[73]

The vital community begun under Gray continued to flourish under Coolbaugh. In addition to woodland camps, students began to form teams in sports such as polo, tennis, football, and baseball.[74] Baseball was particularly popular, and town teams played the Holderness School teams on Saturday afternoons.[75] A student writer describes 1888 games against the Plymouth team with commendable spirit and good sportsmanship: "Although we failed to win, they were very exciting contests, calling forth much applause from the spectators."[76]

The school retained a strong relationship with military families, as it had in its first years. Parents could choose to have their children "fitted for College, the United States Naval and Military Academies at Annapolis and West Point, and the higher Scientific Schools."[77] In fact, Coolbaugh considered "instruction in military tactics [to be] an integral part of the physical training the boys receive."[78] An outgrowth of this belief was the institution of the cadet corps in 1886.[79] This organization was drilled regularly by Major Frank Russell, "an enthusiastic retired West Pointer," but was not enthusiastically embraced by all students.[80] In the student publication The Volunteer, one editorialist complains:

> The chief fault found with the drill is, that the time is taken out of that part of the afternoon given for recreation [...]. If the drill is such an important feature, why not take it out of the school hours, in which case it would become a pleasure, instead of a burden."[81]

Though the drills were sometimes held early in the morning, and sometimes in the afternoon, the cadet corps remained a fixture during all of Coolbaugh's time at the school.[82]

Holderness students—then as now—somehow found time to augment their athletic and academic pursuits with various clubs and activities. During Coolbaugh's tenure, extra-curricular opportunities grew to include at least three literary organizations (the Holderness School Gazette, The Volunteer, and the Ollapodrida), a Camera Club, an Electric Club, five different musical organizations, and several different "secret societies" (fraternities).[83]

Local walks and amusements still held a draw as well. One student recalled "the Frog Pond over on the corner of the grounds on the road to Squam, and the galaxy of little turtles I corralled there and had in a basin in my alcove."[84] Others fondly praised the friendliness of neighboring families. In particular, the Colley farm just past Trinity Church "was the hangout for all the boys for pancakes and pies."[85] Mrs. Colley was an excellent cook, and "would make up a batch of griddle cakes for a matter of 50¢ for a couple of boys, with all the butter, sugar or maple syrup that one wanted, no small matter with growing youngsters!"[86]

High spirits remained a characteristic of Holderness School students, and pranks were common. One outbreak of mischief had stealthy students rubbing classmates' faces with burnt cork in the middle of the night, and resulted in a dire warning printed in the student paper:

> It seems a good place here to say a word to these fellows who cannot sleep o' nights and caper about the dormitory after lights. When the whole dormitory loses their permissions for the week, and are put on bounds for the misde-meanors of a few, who will not keep their beds at the proper time it becomes a bore and will not long be tolerated by those who have no share in making the disturbance. Let these young men have a care, or they may be visited them-selves by those they have placed under such obligations to them, and have to pay the penalty of their sins in a manner that may not be agreeable.[87]

Being put 'on bounds' was a disciplinary action that continued for more than a century at Holderness School. It involved restricting a student's movements to a certain perimeter around school property, and was extremely effective. One stu-dent during Coolbaugh's time observed condemned classmates viewing the for-bidden territory "with longing eyes" because they were "bound down to fifteen acres, while all the surrounding country beckons to them to come and enjoy its freshness."[88]

There seemed to be an astonishing array of activities available to students, given that the school was feeling financial pressures. However, the student body was well-shielded from these pressures. While the trustees appropriately con-cerned themselves with the school's bank account, those living on campus simply continued to draw on seemingly unlimited supplies of energy and creativity.

The size of the campus community waxed and waned during Coolbaugh's time. In his first two years, the number of students rose from fifty-nine to eighty-one.[89] This was a tight fit even in the new dormitory, where a few older boys had enclosed rooms but most students lived in small niches called 'alcoves:'[90]

> My alcove was in the North Dormitory, a drape for a door and all open on top. We had a long iron sink in a wash room with twelve agate bowls. Each alcove contained a bureau, bed and chair.[91]

At the peak of enrollment under Coolbaugh, one student noted that "there is not another alcove or even a closet where another boy could be placed."[92] However, this was not a lasting problem: enrollment slowly declined to forty-nine by 1892, Coolbaugh's last year.[93]

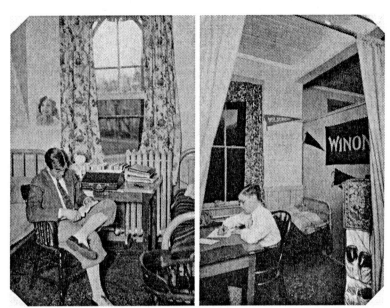

Upper form dorm room (left) and alcove (right) in Knowlton Hall, circa 1929

The enrollment numbers probably reflected the amount of wear that was beginning to show on campus. Trustees spent board meetings discussing "the necessity of making repairs in the residence building and [...] the general condition of the school."[94] However, they took seriously the debt burden for the building of Knowlton Hall, and they did not feel that they could make money available for improvements.

Although no significant additions to the campus could be made during Coolbaugh's tenure, some changes were made possible through the generosity of donors. In particular, the Chapel of the Holy Cross received several significant gifts. A pipe organ made by George H. Hutchins of Boston was donated by the school's alumni (or 'Old Boys') in 1890, as were a new altar and reredos. In Coolbaugh's last year, the chapel received a gift of a processional cross, and friends of the Balch family gave stained glass windows of St. Agnes and St. Cecilia in memory of Emily Balch and her daughter.[95]

It is clear that, despite financial restraints, school life continued to deepen and become richer under Coolbaugh. Although he returned to the Midwest in 1892 and resumed a life of pastoral work, Coolbaugh never forgot his ties to Holderness School. He visited campus in later years to tell students stories of the school's beginnings,[96] and maintained a warm correspondence with some of the Holderness School trustees until his death in 1921.[97]

A year before he passed away, a humble Coolbaugh took stock of fifty years of ordained life and wrote the following words:

> It is not without misgivings and unutterable regrets that I take full or partial retrospects of the one half century. So much more might have [been] done otherwise and to better and fuller advantage to others [or] the Mother Church and less to self-ease and comfort. [But] my years have all been happy if not fruitful of good and holy works.[98]

Certainly Coolbaugh's time at Holderness School constituted a good work, one which was appreciated by all who knew him. With the end of his headmastership, the school concluded a period that had successfully established the institution's roots. The school would enter a new era during the next headmaster's tenure, developing both unique traditions and a reputation for excellence.

1892–1922: REV. LORIN WEBSTER

Rev. Lorin Webster had been associated with the Holderness School long before becoming its third headmaster. A graduate of St. Paul's School, Trinity College, and Berkeley Divinity School, Webster spent a year on the Holderness School faculty under headmaster Gray before leaving to become rector of St. Mark's Parish in Ashland.[99] He was a natural educator, known to be a "strict man, but fair, respected, and liked by the boys."[100]

When Webster rejoined Holderness School in 1892, a flurry of activity followed in his wake; board minutes during his first years are filled with lists of the campus improvements and repairs to be effected. It appears that Webster had a keen mind for managing to make such improvements on a budget. One of Webster's teachers described him as a "rare business manager who made a dollar go as far as any one could,"[101] and the trustees also seemed to recognize this aptitude. They quickly rescinded a motion that had previously restricted control of business affairs to the board's treasurer.[102] The headmaster and the members of the board instead forged a partnership, and together undertook the long process of carrying campus work to completion.

These improvements—which in part included electric light, steam heat, new Schoolhouse floors and desks, and foundation fixes to Knowlton Hall—did not come cheaply.[103] For many years, Webster and the trustees struggled to find the delicate balance between expense outlay and a return on their investments. Their efforts were successful within a relatively short period of time. By 1896, Webster proclaimed his satisfaction to the trustees, stating that the "present condition of the school [...] proved to be more encouraging than in any previous year of his administration."[104] As they had hoped, financial security soon followed the school's physical well-being. A gradual economic improvement led to treasurer's reports that trustees described as "highly encouraging" and "gratifying." In one1905 trustee meeting, cash on hand of $1,435.93 was reported, and the minutes note gleefully that "all were highly pleased at the excellent showing."[105]

What makes these early successes doubly impressive is that they were achieved in conjunction with Webster's administration of a thriving academic and residential life. Described as a "fine scholar" who was "a painstaking and able teacher, particularly in English,"[106] Webster nevertheless seemed to leave his mark most powerfully in the extra-curricular areas.

Webster's personal affinity for music influenced school life. A published musician[107], he composed a school song[108] and a piece to be sung at school baseball games.[109] Webster also conducted and arranged music for the successful Holderness School choir, which performed regularly on and off campus. Not surprisingly, musical societies and clubs flourished throughout his time at the school.

But music was not necessary Webster's only love. As Edric Weld put it, "[Webster's] interest in the choir was surpassed only by his interest in athletics." Webster embraced athletics as an important aspect of a healthy school life, an outlook that resonates on campus to this day. His approach seemed to come at the right time, for a fresh perspective was now finding voice at trustee meetings. The young Alumni Association had elected a representative trustee, Dr. William Hubbard, who told the board that he believed the school would be more attractive to boys if it could offer athletic equipment, lectures, and other entertainments.[110]

The board listened. In 1902, the campus was graded, and a baseball diamond, football gridiron, and quarter-mile running track were laid out.[111] Webster raised the roof of the "temporary gym" (which had been in use from around 1887) to allow for basketball games, and at the same time put in two dirt tennis courts.[112] Dinner hour was moved up to allow for daylight athletic practices.[113] It is no surprise, with these encouragements, that "interscholastic sports came into their own."[114] Football, basketball, baseball, hockey, and track teams all began competing successfully against outside teams.

Holderness School baseball team, 1889

Holderness School football team, 1897

Organized team sports were not the only athletic pastimes pursued by Holderness School students, as classic New England outdoor winter activities still held their allure. Although skiing was not a recognized sport during this era, the seeds of interest were being sown. An alumnus from the class of 1918 recalled its first appearance on the Holderness School campus:

> Thomas Crosbie '17 came to school the fall of 1915, having spent the previous winter in Switzerland. He had learned to ski and soon interested a half-dozen of us in joining him. [...] [In] the winters of 1915 through 1918, there was skiing at Holderness, based on a Swiss technique.[115]

The expansion of outdoor athletic amenities was followed closely by the improvement of other facilities. A pressing reason to expand the main school building had been developing for several years:

> Holderness School, unlike many other educational institutions, is supposed to live within its income—and that not a very large one. As a result masters do not stay long. The initial compensation is large enough to attract good inexperienced men. But our masters soon find much better positions elsewhere—when they do not enter the ministry. Then there is no accommodation here for a married master. It is to be hoped that the [School can erect] a modest lodging for wedded pedagogues.[116]

Although financial questions had been holding back development, the trustees felt that the school's financial well-being was stabilizing. This, combined with the need to improve faculty retention, made the time seem right to expand Knowlton Hall by constructing an addition that included room for married faculty and other amenities.[117] In 1908, the trustees approved a $16,000 mortgage, and the new wing was built.[118] The expansion coincided with the peak of enrollment under Webster, with seventy-five students at the school.

The alumni, meanwhile, were attempting to raise funds for the construction of a new gymnasium. Although the project was kicked off in 1906, and architectural plans were donated by an alumnus, the Old Boys were unable to secure enough contributions to cover construction.[119] The project languished for several years until, in 1912, a gift from the estate of a former trustee provided the funds to complete the project.[120] The new Carpenter Memorial Gymnasium, containing both academic and athletic facilities, was described in the school catalog as follows:

> The main building is 82 ft. long and 38 ft. wide, and, besides the laboratories already mentioned, contains a recitation room, the Physical Director's office, a locker-room, a toilet and shower bath room, a billiard room, and a room for storing furniture. There is a running-track, which also serves as a balcony for

watching basket-ball games and athletic exhibitions, and a stage for lectures, concerts, and dramatics. A trophy-room and all the other accessories of a modern gymnasium have been provided.[121]

The new amenities had a happy effect on the school. Webster reported to the trustees in 1914 that "the tone of the school had never been higher during his administration and that the spirit of study was earnest and scholarly."[122] Students were successful in the classroom and on the playing fields, and the trustees in turn reassured Webster that letters from parents and college presidents all expressed pleasure with the results of a Holderness School education.[123]

Sadly, the events of the First World War would have a sobering impact upon the school. Long-time trustees were called to service, and were replaced with difficulty.[124] Wartime (and post-war) prices rose, while enrollment dropped, and the trustees were forced to borrow more money to cover expenses.[125] In 1917, the board raised tuition with the understanding that it "be reduced to the former amount as soon as conditions allow;" such conditions did not present themselves, and tuition was raised twice more in the following two years.[126]

As in previous lean times, however, campus life continued with spirit. Students wrote patriotic editorials in school publications, and competed as vigorously as ever in athletic matches. The fraternities that were begun under Rev. Coolbaugh thrived, and had meeting rooms on the top floor of the 'Old Gym.' Invitations to social events were exchanged between students at Holderness School and the girls attending the Plymouth Normal School or St. Mary's School in Concord.

In short, life continued, and the school—together with the rest of the country—weathered the difficult times with courage. When the end of the war came, as one student remembered, the school community greeted the news with relief and joy:

> On the evening of 11 November 1918, during supper, the rector, Dr. Lorin Webster, was called to the telephone. When he returned to the dining room in old Livermore Hall, he knocked on a glass for silence and announced, 'Boys, I have wonderful news. The war is over. An armistice was declared at eleven o'clock this morning.' I [Neil Pierce] became jet-propelled, ran out of the dining-room and up the path to the schoolhouse. There I proceeded to ring the bell. I managed three to four tolls, then turned the bell over. It was thereafter silent until a man came out from Plymouth to repair it.[127]

At the time of the armistice, Webster had been headmaster of Holderness School for over twenty-five years. He would remain for another five years, only leaving the school to join his son at Peking University in 1922.[128] Though the school has since been fortunate in having several headmasters who offered decades of service, Webster was the first of this rare breed.

At the time of Webster's retirement, the campus reflected his own interests as a scholar-athlete-musician, and this was to be a lasting legacy. Webster's were no easy shoes to fill. One former student described the influence Webster wielded:

> [The] longer I have been out, and the more I have learned of other schools, the more do I now appreciate the decisive influence that Dr. Lorin Webster and his amazingly strong staff of teachers had over my choice of scholarship as a life interest. He was a very great school man; a scholar, a gentleman, and a Christian. His long, unwearying patience with me deserved far greater appreciation than my stubborn youth was able or willing to give him.[129]

The difficulty in finding a worthy successor, combined with the same financial concerns that had dogged the school for decades, worried the trustees. They discussed a temporary closing of the school, but decided against the move.[130] Determined to remain open, the trustees began the search for a new headmaster. In the meantime, they gave thanks to Webster for the impressive work that he had accomplished on their behalf:

> The Trustees of Holderness School [...] desire to express their appreciation of the untiring zeal and earnestness with which Dr. Webster and Mrs. Webster have given themselves to the service and welfare of the School for thirty years. There have been heavy burdens of anxiety and responsibility which they have borne, and laborious details of work which they have cheerfully undertaken. Thirty years of service as Rector of Holderness School means a record of devoted work for Christian education which is unusual in its length and in the demands of willing service which it involves.[131]

No better tribute to the man can be written today.

1922–1928: Rev. R. Eliot Marshall

The trustees were successful in their search for Lorin Webster's successor, hiring Rev. R. Eliot Marshall to be the school's fourth headmaster in 1922. As others had before him, Marshall began his work at Holderness School by improving the school grounds. After his first summer, students returned to changes that included new bathrooms with showers ("plenty of hot water may be found there at all times"), fresh paint, updates to library furniture, a new tennis court, re-set goal posts, and new Schoolhouse lighting fixtures.[132] This was more than simple house cleaning. The school had not had substantial renovations for a decade, and Marshall's fresh eyes saw "that the run-down condition of the property was a drawback to the success of the school."[133] By improving the appearance of campus, he hoped to enhance the school's future prospects.

Though nominally Marshall had the support of the trustees in these efforts, the board was entering a new era of responsibility. The Diocese—now focused on missionary duties—considered the school to be a basically independent entity, and the trustees began "to regard their function rather that of keeping the Rector from spending too much money that that of providing it for him."[134] With money tight, Marshall was soon forced to focus on improvements that could be made without serious financial impact on the school.

He did so by concentrating his attention on the heart of the school: the students. Himself a product of "an intellectual family of the best traditions," Marshall encouraged the boys to focus more on their coursework, and less on athletics.[135] His foreword to one edition of the school paper was perhaps representative of his views on the subject:

> In athletics we are having a good time, keeping our standards high, trying to maintain a proper balance between studies and sports, remaining utterly and purposely indifferent to the question whether or not we gain publicity by having winning teams, but tremendously concerned that our games shall be earnestly, cleanly, courteously played, and that we can take defeat with as much equanimity as we can win victory. It would be easy to admit ten or a dozen semi-professional athletes to the School,—they apply for admission and even for pay every fall with the regularity of tides and 'bills payable,'—but they will not be accepted. We shall remain lovers of sport,—amateurs.[136]

Marshall's strategies were to strengthen academic requirements (athletes were not allowed to play if they were on academic probation[137]) and to use positive reinforcement (extra vacation days were awarded for good grades and conduct[138]).

This focus on academics was not myopic. Marshall hoped to improve Holderness School's academic reputation because "the success of our graduates in college and in business is our best advertisement."[139] He believed that this type of advertising would attract more students and result in a more solid financial standing for the school. He enjoyed success in building up the school's academic strengths, and reported to the trustees that "the School was being more favorably regarded by college entrance committees and would increasingly take its place among good schools."[140]

However, the school under Marshall was by no means a quiet, scholarly enclave. Marshall also took it upon himself to re-energize school spirit, changing the school colors from crimson and white (too close to the colors of nearby St. Paul's School for comfort, one suspects) to the proud blue and silver still in use today. The new colors were taken from the coat of arms of the Earl of Holderness, and the school paper reported that it was "the recollection of some of the Trustees [...] that the original, or at least early, colors of the school were [the blue and silver] now used."[141]

Sports uniforms were changed to reflect the new colors. Hockey gained prominence after an impromptu game against Plymouth High School was held during the Plymouth Carnival:

> It was at this time that the need for a hockey rink [at Holderness School] became pressing. It was therefore with great enthusiasm that the suggestion to flood the old gym was received. By one morning of constant work by several of the students the floor was cleared. To flood the gym was more of a problem as the water had to be carried in pails from the main building. After it had been flooded three times the ice was ready to be skated on.[142]

The popularity of basketball also increased, leading one student to emphatically state in 1926 that "[it] is a known fact that basketball is the leading sport at Holderness."[143] Student enthusiasm had apparently survived a cancelled basketball schedule the previous year (the campus had been under quarantine for scarlet fever).[144]

Other activities and traditions were coming into being as well. Marshall and the school matron, Mrs. Tyack, began a new custom in which "[every] boy who has a birthday during school sessions is presented with a birthday cake."[145] Although school enrollment numbers are significantly higher, the school's kitchen staff still presents cake to students with birthdays on one day each month. Another well-known Holderness School tradition was begun in the fall of 1922, when The Dial began its impressively long print run.[146] Published as a school newspaper during its first year, The Dial quickly changed to a magazine format, and did not convert to the now-familiar format of annual yearbook until around 1940.

House parties had become an established routine at Holderness School by Marshall's time. Visiting girls would lodge nearby with chaperones and stay throughout the weekend, taking part in a schedule of events held at the school. A typical schedule might include an athletic game on Friday night, followed by "informal dancing and singing." A variety of activities were offered during the day on Saturday, and winter gatherings in particular afforded numerous activities for participants to enjoy:

> There was plenty of fine snow for snow-shoeing, skiing, tobogganing, and all sorts of winter sports, and everyone entered eagerly into them. Owing to the ingenuity of some of the boys, there was a splendid toboggan slide, a real thriller, and a ski-jump to add to the excitement of the sports.[147]

A formal dance was usually held on Saturday night, with more outdoor activities filling the time on Sunday until guests had to depart.[148]

Flooded train depot (left) and residential street (right) in the town of Plymouth, 1936

Girls from the Plymouth Normal School and the town of Plymouth were frequent guests at house parties and school dances. In fact, the school maintained a happy relationship with all of the neighboring towns. Whether fighting forest fires in Campton[149] or moving furniture from flooded homes in Plymouth[150], boys at Holderness School did their best to extend a helping hand. The good will was returned in kind:

> In a basketball game between Holderness and Ashland, an incident occurred which we think rather significant. A number of Plymouth High school boys accompanied out team to the game. During the contest they supported our boys. At the finish they surrounded them and left the hall singing a Holderness song. Some of the Plymouth students had opposed our team in a series of two hotly contested games a few evenings before. [...] With such a fine example [of spirit and cooperation] given by Plymouth, we of Holderness will do our bit. Now, we merely say, 'Hats off to Plymouth.'[151]

'Town and gown' conflicts were not in evidence, and the school was truly intent upon integrating with the greater community.

It is clear that school life was still vital and energetic during this time. Indeed, Marshall had succeeded in refocusing the school's energies toward academics without sacrificing athletic achievements or spirit. However, he still deeply felt the financial pressures facing the school. Marshall wanted nothing more than to concentrate on the "minds and souls" of his boys, and in 1926 he told the trustees that "I devoutly hope that the time is not far distant when financial worries can be eliminated and my spirit freed to do better work in these most important fields."[152]

The Bishop tried to allay his concerns, writing:

> You have done so splendidly in bringing up the morale and numbers of the School, and are so putting us on the way to self-support, that it seems too bad that you should have any bother or worry about finances. You must leave that heavy burden to me, co-operating as I know you will do, by economizing wherever possible. [...] I am a sordid soul, just at present, that has little interest in religion or morals, and is wholly wrapped up in pondering about water for the showers and toilets, warm vegetables and conditions that the cook will approve, wash tubs and a drying room for winter.[153]

The trustees did what they could to help, and repeatedly commended Marshall for his accomplishments at the school. However, the headmaster increasingly felt unequal to balancing the tasks of securing higher enrollment, managing financial questions, and performing his campus duties.[154] In 1928 Marshall, who had "devoted himself to making school life more happy for the boys in whom he took a deep personal interest," retired from the school and returned to parish work.[155]

1929–1931: REV. ALBAN RICHEY

During the transition period after Marshall's resignation, the board had difficulty locating an appropriate candidate for his replacement. Faculty member Herbert Carpenter stepped in as acting headmaster for the1928–1929 academic year.[156] The trustees hired Rev. Alban Richey midway through that year, and following a few school visits, Richey arrived on campus to assume his new role in the fall of 1929.

The new headmaster brought an entirely different approach to the school than had Marshall. Richey joined the school at a time when the financial burden of the school was nearing $60,000, and a reduction had been made in the money made available for scholarships.[157] The headmaster and the trustees knew that the enrollment numbers had to be raised if the school was to be kept open. Rather than focusing on internal academic changes, Richey felt that the school's profile could be raised if energies were turned outward.

The board was impressed and revitalized by this vision. New Hampshire Governor Winant, who had been a member of the board since 1923, was soon joined by other notable personages.[158] These included Richey's former senior warden Franklin D. Roosevelt, and in 1929 "Holderness had at the celebration of its Fiftieth the distinction of having on its board the Governor of New Hampshire, the Governor of New York, as well as two bishops [...] and Justice Peaslee of the New Hampshire Supreme Court."[159]

At Richey's urging, the board pursued the idea of advertising, which they had first considered in 1925. Already advertising in various church magazines, in 1930 the school purchased additional column space in Cosmopolitan, Red Book, Harper's, Harper's Bazaar, and Good Housekeeping magazines.[160] Bishop Dallas was not altogether comfortable with this new approach, but realized "something must be done to bring back the good will of the school" and approved the move. Richey supplemented this advertising by publishing two school view books with photographs of "Life at the School" and "Winter Sports and Outdoor Life."[161]

The committed new rector carried out two fresh strategies for connecting with more prospective students. First, he increased the practice of exchanging sermons with other congregations, thereby raising awareness of the school. In November of his first year alone, Richey preached at Laconia and Norwich and hosted the Lord Bishop of Aberdeen at Holderness School.[162] He also preached outside of the Diocese of New Hampshire, making engagements in New Jersey, Delaware, New York, and Massachusetts.[163] Second, Richey reached out to the school's young alumni base and encouraged them to support their alma mater. When the

Fiftieth anniversary approached, Richey visited meetings of the Old Boys, show-ing films of school life so as to "revive their interest and stimulate their desire to attend this reunion."[164] This was a successful venture, and on June 10 of 1930, the celebrating alumni "formed a permanent Alumni organization."[165] Such organizations had been formed before, but never at the suggestion of the school and its trustees. Richey facilitated continuing contact with this organization by producing the first Holderness School Alumni Bulletins.[166]

While convinced of the urgency surrounding the need for expanded public support, Richey did not neglect the campus. He made improvements when he could, focusing on areas where a relatively small change could make a large visual impact. The Schoolhouse went from red paint to cream with green trim, and the interior of Knowlton Hall was painted so that it "gleams and glistens most invit-ingly to the stranger seeking knowledge."[167] He thankfully accepted Governor Winant's donation of a driveway and turning space, along with trees, shrubs and flowerbeds planted throughout the campus.[168] By taking care not to neglect such cosmetic changes, Richey helped to raise morale; meanwhile, he continued to work with the board to meet the larger equipment needs and make more substan-tial renovations to Knowlton Hall.

By the spring of 1930, Richey had succeeded in smartening up the campus, raising public awareness of the school, and bringing together a strong alumni base. In many ways, students were flourishing as they had for years—competing athletically, producing school magazines, celebrating special events. But as head-master Weld later pointed out, the school at that point had "everything but boys."[169] To remedy this, Richey and his assistant drew on the first fruits of the school's advertising and recruited heavily. By the following fall, student enroll-ment had increased from forty to sixty-seven.

The drastic increase in enrollment presented "a ticklish problem in assimila-tion" and Richey was faced with many disciplinary problems in the 1930–1931 academic year.[170] To help create more structure in residential life, Richey insti-tuted a system whereby the students were divided into three 'clubs' (Knowlton, Carpenter, and Livermore), which competed for points. The forms were evenly distributed between the clubs, and each club had a faculty advisor and student officers. Richey felt that the club system "develops the tendency to make everyone pull for his personal honor and for his club, thereby augmenting the spirit of fel-lowship and cooperation. [...] Everyone is on an even basis."[171] The first boys were initiated into these clubs on Halloween of 1930, following school celebra-tions at a controlled thirty-foot bonfire.[172]

It should perhaps be noted that uncontrolled fires occurred relatively frequently at this time. As in the past, students offered their services as fire fighters when necessary, maintaining strong ties to the communities surrounding the school. When one 1930 fire in Plymouth burned an entire block, students from Holderness School went down to help fight it back, and the school itself held fire drills on a regular basis.[173] This experience may have paid off in January of 1931, when a fire broke out in Knowlton Hall. The Dial describes the event as follows:

> Monday night while we were eating supper some one rushed into the dining room with the news that the school was on fire. Those boys who had been appointed to operate fire extinguishers in case of a fire rushed to get them and then hurried up to the East Dorm where the fire was raging. Immediately, it was seen that the fire might get away, and the boys who roomed in the East Dorm began taking their clothes and their belongings out. While some of the fellows were fighting the fire, others were removing the furniture from Mr. Richey's apartment. Everything was taken over to the gym. The firemen of Plymouth were notified of the fire and shortly afterward the firemen and the apparatus arrived. The work of the firemen was made harder than usual because of a snow storm.[174]

As they had so many years earlier, Plymouth residents generously housed boys who had been burned out. The trustees extended vacation by two weeks while repairs were made, and then school life resumed. A month later yet another fire alarm was raised at the school, but it turned out to be only a mattress burning behind the gym.[175]

There is no evidence of what caused either of these unhappy incidents. They may have been accidental, or they may have been acts of arson. It may be simplistic to attribute the fires to an unsettled student body. However, it does seem that, like headmaster Marshall before him, Richey saw a conflict between his responsibilities to the students and his efforts to act strategically for the school. Financial restraints yet again were checking progress on the latter, and Richey went to the board with his concerns. Underscoring the immediacy of the problem, he stated that "we all are aware that in order to insure the future funds are needed at this very moment" and asked for the trustees' support:

> If [the Rector's] job, in addition to the very necessary constructive work of both an intangible and tangible character which concentrates itself about such a position, and at such a time in history of the school when a large part of his time must be spent at the school, is to provide an endowment for the school, or to secure the funds to pay the deficit incurred yearly while the school is

small in number, then the Rector must not only honestly disagree with this opinion, but also express his very apparent inability to do so […].[176]

Richey had a warm relationship with the board, and after pointing out his concerns, he continued to work with them to outline strategies for the school's success. However, after securing high enrollment numbers during the 1930–1931 academic year, Richey decided to move on. It is remarkable that, despite being headmaster of Holderness School for only two years, Richey imparted a vision that had a lasting impact on both the board and the school.

1931–1951: REV. EDRIC A. WELD

During the search for the school's next headmaster, Bishop Dallas approached Rev. Edric A. Weld. Weld had been a candidate for the position in 1928 as well, and he later joked that with more experience, he "would not have acted on the supposition that if a bishop asks you twice, you ought to say yes."[177] In fact, he approached the challenge with seriousness and dedication. Weld "brought to the school a warm and charismatic personality, a devotion to education and excellence, and an inexhaustible abundance of personal generosity and commitment."[178]

Weld also brought high hopes to the school, and had the strong support of Bishop Dallas and the board of trustees. But after only a month in his new position, he faced a terrible challenge when Knowlton Hall—still the school's sole residential building—burned to the ground. Weld later wrote about the experience:

> The hopes which had flourished in October of 1930 shrivelled to ashes along with the interior of Knowlton Hall in October, 1931. Trustees awoke to discover that the mortgage, which had been allowed to mount with each successive deficit practically to the height of the flames as they burst from the roof, now would consume all the fire insurance money. Faculty members found themselves without their children's clothes, and many possessions. The boys in the West Wing had been able to do a thorough salvage job. The boys in the North Dormitory had in some cases been dragged from bed, and had nothing but what they wore. The rector's silver and pictures had been handed out the windows, and the grand piano dragged minus legs by members of the football squad through the main floor. The books were all gone.[179]

Showing the same generosity that had prevailed in previous years, residents of Plymouth welcomed students into their homes until the boys could return to their families.

Thanks to the spirited willingness of the thirty-eight students and their parents, the school re-opened only a week later.[180] The trustees arranged for lodging and classrooms to be set up in the Pemigewasset House, then a hotel in Plymouth, but the school's athletic fields and the Chapel remained in use. Drawbacks to the new provisions were balanced by some excellent benefits, including the "Pemi's" close proximity to (all-girl) Plymouth Normal School, the use of the hotel's ballroom facilities for dances, and the fact that every pair of rooms had its own bathroom.[181]

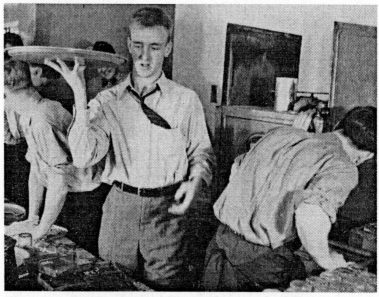

Students participating in the "self-help" job program, 1937

Meanwhile, the trustees and the headmaster had to make the serious decision of whether to close the school at the end of the year, or rebuild the campus. They were only willing to rebuild if the school could stay true to its original ideal: "to combine the highest degree of excellence in instruction and care-taking with the lowest possible charge for tuition and board."[182] In order to stay open while adhering to these principles, the trustees constructed a plan that involved some changes. First, the school's tuition was to stay the same, but the physical plant would be increased to a size that could accommodate one hundred students. Second, a "self-help" program like that at Kent School would be instituted; work-scholarships were eliminated, and instead every student would have equal shares in campus work.[183]

New campus plans were drawn up by Jens Fredrick Larson, and the projected price tag for required buildings and endowment was an intimidating $640,000.[184] Even with donations reaching the $100,000 mark by spring, the trustees were concerned about the advisability of undertaking such a project.[185] This was not a surprising perspective, as the nation was in the midst of its great economic Depression. However, Weld assured the board that he himself would bear the responsibility of meeting any deficit, and the trustees voted to continue. It was a defining moment for the school. Those trustees who could not see their way to condoning the decision resigned; all remaining trustees dedicated themselves to the school's renewal.[186]

It was not an easy road to take. The appeal of the new buildings did not have impact as quickly as expected, and enrollment suffered.[187] When, according to the building plan, the time came to build the new dormitory, it seemed illogical and possibly even ill-advised. Weld later recalled that "to go ahead and build a dormitory, when the small temporary rooms in Livermore were not all filled, required perhaps an even greater venture of faith than the building of Livermore."[188] But build it the trustees did. Their faith was rewarded by a steady increase in enrollment over the next years, and the stabilization of the school that had yet again come so close to closing its doors. Under Weld's leadership, the school again began to prosper.

More challenges arose with the onset of World War II, and these were met with dignity and spirit. The school deferred its building plans at that time, instead asking for contributions to a special scholarship fund for child refugees from Europe.[189] By September of 1940, the school was hosting three English boys and two German refugees as a part of its own war work;[190] it also invited two Japanese-American students from American relocation centers.[191] In the summers, the school lent the campus to a program called *American Seminar*, which helped "acclimatize refugee scholars to teach in American Institutions."[192]

Students also enthusiastically undertook relief work. Two student leaders garnered one hundred percent student body participation in a clothing drive organized through *Young America Wants to Help*.[193] Multiple school plays and concerts were given to support war relief, and these raised enough money to send an ambulance to Britain bearing the school's name.[194] The school also reached out to former students, distributing a small, easily portable booklet of prayers to alumni; it was "dedicated to the class of 1943 and to all former members of Holderness School now in the armed services of their country."[195]

As the war drew to a close, the school maintained close contact with its graduates. Weld distributed addresses of enlisted alumni in Europe, "in the hope that it will make it possible for them to correspond with each other if they have months of waiting for redeployment."[196] In May of 1945, a special service of honor was held at the school for the thirteen alumni known to be missing or killed in action; over half of this number had graduated within the past five years.[197] Weld's daughter later recalled the impact of the losses, and wrote, "I can't emphasize enough how that war influenced everyone at the school."[198] A lasting reminder of the sacrifices of Holderness School alumni still remains in the Chapel of the Holy Cross, where eight stained glass windows designed by Charles J. Connick Associates in Boston memorialize some of the fallen.

The school emerged from the war saddened by loss, but with optimism for the future. Faculty who had been in service during the war returned to the school, and alumni servicemen also came to visit campus.[199] Residential life continued with many established traditions in tact. Students still took part in volunteer firefighting, as had been common under previous headmasters.[200] The custom of taking a headmaster's holiday from school to explore nearby peaks became a regular practice:

> [An] institution that had an especial flavor during the thirties was Mountain Day. The school was small enough and the faculty young enough for all to go; only the rare football cripple stayed behind with 'Mom' Holbrook, or later with Mrs. Petty. The earliest mountain days were made doubly significant because Bishop Dallas climbed with us, and afterward invited everyone to Bethlehem for refreshments.[201]

Late in Weld's tenure, a similar tradition called "Cranmore Days" began. This referred to a three-day outing to Cranmore Mountain in North Conway, where the entire school enjoyed skiing and skating. As had Bishop Dallas before him, Bishop Hall participated enthusiastically in these events.[202]

Holderness School athletic teams continued to dominate, with students beginning to embrace winter sports as a new form of competitive exercise. House party celebrations continued but, for financial reasons, became single day events rather than full weekends.[203] The school also began to explore new areas of interest during Weld's tenure. Visual arts flourished, with the school adding a craft shop, an art studio, and dedicated arts faculty.[204] Music thrived, with more than half of the school taking part in the Glee Club.[205] Gilbert and Sullivan musical productions came into their heyday, as well, and continued to be an annual theatrical tradition for almost twenty-five years.[206] In addition to new activities in the fine arts, other extra-curriculars sprang up. A debate club was formed and began to earn a solid reputation; by 1949, it boasted twenty-one members.[207] Student Robert Creeley, who would go on to become an award-winning poet and author, began a new student newspaper called The Bull.[208] This paper would have several reincarnations, appearing on campus at intervals until the 1980s. It was a vibrant and busy campus.

In 1949, the school made an important modification to student life. At that time, the students voted to adopt the Proctor Plan and the House Plan, which gave increased responsibility to the student body. Under the new plans, student leaders were chosen by their peers each year based on their "leadership, dependability, fairness and initiative,"[209] and then became responsible for managing the jobs program, the dorms, and some disciplinary decisions. This new government had "the advantage of developing the maximum amount of student responsibility, a minimum of penalties, and a minimum of friction between faculty and students."[210] It was enormously successful, and is still employed at the school today.

While school life rolled along, the post-war economy forced the trustees to face rising costs and questions about how to meet them. Although the personal generosity of the Weld family had smoothed the school's way through many such challenges, financial concerns were intensifying. Weld advised the trustees that the best course would be to raise tuition to an amount approaching that of similar schools.[211] This would avoid the need to reduce the number of student scholarships, and would allow the school to provide adequate compensation to retain experienced faculty members. Weld believed strongly that, while modest Holderness School could not "have the laboratories or library or outside speakers or some of the beautiful adornments of the larger schools [...] we can have as good teachers man for man."[212]

This approach was adopted, and some of the financial pressures on the school were alleviated. However, Weld was approaching a self-imposed twenty-year limit to his tenure.[213] Having shepherded the school through trials that included a burned campus, the Depression, and World War II, Weld was ready to pass on the responsibilities of a new era to an energized successor. Weld informed the trustees of his desire to find "a young and dynamic man to replace him and to carry on the fine tradition of the school which has since been its foundation—excellence in scholarship, character, good health, and a rugged life."[214]

Those who knew Weld remember him with an astonishing degree of pride and affection. For twenty years and more, he embodied the very principles that he hoped to instill in his students: faith, perseverance, and generosity. "Professorial in manner and absent-mindedness," Weld's outward appearance disguised a man who had the vision and fortitude to see the school through perilous times.[215] Holderness School owes its present existence in great part to his work, and that legacy will not soon be forgotten.

1951–1977: DONALD C. HAGERMAN

In his final report to the trustees, Edric Weld stated "my conviction that the time has come for new life, new imagination, new energy at the head [...]. I can already see in my successor my hopes for the future being realized."[216] Donald C. Hagerman had been selected as the next headmaster of Holderness School. A young protégé of Deerfield's famous headmaster Frank L. Boyden, Hagerman was a Dartmouth alumnus who came to Holderness School via Deerfield, Tabor, and the Clark School, where he had been headmaster. Along with his wife Elizabeth ("Ibba"), he brought a wealth of new ideas and a vigorous commitment to the school.

Hagerman was also the first Holderness School headmaster not to be an ordained minister. The trustees felt "the new head should have a strong background of educational experience" and, barring discovery of a clergyman with the appropriate credentials, they believed that hiring a layman was perfectly appropriate.[217] In particular, they hoped to find a new head with "high character and a youthful aggressive spirit," and this Hagerman had in abundance.[218]

At the helm for twenty-six years, Hagerman oversaw many changes at the school. Some of these changes were strategically planned as being in the school's best interest; some came about as a result of tumultuous and often difficult times in the nation's history. All of the changes informed the development of the school, which was moving into a truly new era in its history.

One of Hagerman's early, carefully planned strategies was to increase the size of the school. In Hagerman's first academic year (1951–52), 72 students were enrolled. By the 1955–56 academic year, he had raised this number to 107 and formed the concrete goal of increasing school size to 125-150.[219] As he explained to the trustees, this target size would still allow "close personal guidance" while avoiding competition with large schools of 400-750. Hagerman argued that staying smaller had negative financial implications and "runs the risk of attracting boys who are incapable of competing successfully in larger schools."[220]

The school continued to gradually adjust the target upward, and over the course of Hagerman's 26 years at the school, enrollment increased to 226 students.[221] As Hagerman's successor Pete Woodward later noted, this feat was most remarkable in that "Holderness lost none of its spirit and togetherness as it grew."[222] The sense of family was retained by keeping campus residences small and home-like. New living space (made necessary by the growth of the school) was added in the form of several new faculty homes; each new building also included space for four to fifteen students. By choosing to take this route instead of building a few large, impersonal dormitory buildings, Hagerman preserved—and celebrated—the close relationship between students and teachers that had exemplified Holderness life to that point.

Campus construction was not cheap, and new dormitories were by no means the only requirements for the expanding school. New classroom space, administrative space, and dining space were all necessary if the school was to properly support its own growth.[223] Raising funds was a daunting task for a school that still had a relatively modest alumni base, but "authentic Holderness angels did appear."[224] Over the course of Hagerman's tenure, new facilities on campus included Weld Hall, a Schoolhouse addition, multiple dormitories (including Rathbun and buildings on Mt. Prospect), the headmaster's residence, Bartsch Athletic Center, and the Jerome Webster Library in Livermore Hall.

While Hagerman prudently planned for the future of the school and its facilities, day to day life was also evolving. Students in Hagerman's early years had come to "a college preparatory school, offering preparation for liberal arts and engineering."[225] As Pat Henderson wrote in her history of the school, this formula for education was soon to be challenged:

> "[In] the late 60s [...] curricular evolution over epochs was replaced by instant revolution. Black, Asian and Canadian history, ecology, science projects, computer work and economics were added to the curriculum. In the classes of the early 70s, some students postponed going to college. Work, travel or a postgraduate year at a school in Europe were looked upon with favor by college admissions officers. In addition, many students spent their summer and holiday vacations traveling to little-known niches of the globe or finding exotic jobs."[226]

Don Henderson with the Trail Crew, 1954

In order to address these new educational needs and to challenge the "general malaise among students in the spring of their senior year," Hagerman introduced the spring study period that would eventually evolve into the school's Senior Projects.[227] He also actively pursued foundation grants and endowments to fund exciting new aspects of academic life. This strategy encouraged fledgling programs like Backward Bound (in which students helped faculty member Bill Clough '57 build a cabin with 19th century tools), the Outing Club, and what is now known as Out Back. Many of these programs carved out a permanent place in the Holderness experience, and continue to generate warm memories for future alumni every year.

By hiring a world-class skiing instructor to continue the winter sports program begun by Weld, Hagerman also ensured that athletics would flourish at Holderness School. Olympic coach Don Henderson helped sculpt not just student athletes, but the physical trails as well. Sports teams flourished with the additional student enrollment, and Hagerman hired wisely to support them. Activities as diverse as lacrosse, rock-climbing, and sailing were all led by motivated and talented coaches.[228] In traditional sports, the informal rivalry that had existed between Holderness School and Proctor Academy since the 1920s became more official. Students looked forward to football matches, in particular, with great anticipation. As one student noted: "Each year the one game Holderness awaits is

Proctor. It is for this the boys sweat out three grueling months of work."[229] During the years of this rivalry, a white football was traditionally presented to the loser of the Holderness-Proctor game each year.[230]

Extra-curricular activities continued to develop as well. The debate team begun under Weld remained competitive throughout the 1950s and 1960s, winning awards and titles.[231] Gilbert and Sullivan productions continued for some years, with students actively involved in set design as well as performance.[232] The school's theatrical performances began to shift to more dramatic fare by the mid-1960s, however, and the Gilbert and Sullivan tradition slowly faded. In the meantime, hands-on activities became increasingly popular with students: the forge got extensive use[233], a woodworking shop was created[234], and a new kiln was donated to the school.[235] Practical interests were also reflected in some of the school's organizations, which included astronomy, electronics, photography, and car clubs.[236] During the winter house party, now termed Winter Carnival, dormitories competed against each other to produce the best snow sculpture. This new tradition was taken quite seriously, as art teacher Herbert Waters later noted:

> In the winter we made a big deal of Snow Sculpture—lighting them at night with colored spots—developing a fierce competition—bringing in outside professional judges, etc. One year one was featured in the New York Times—Eisenhower and Taft pulling a [big] elephant (GOP) in different directions.[237]

While residential life expanded to include new interests, social changes affecting the entire nation were about to face the school. In 1969, Hannah Roberts, the daughter of a faculty member, asked if she might take classes at all-male Holderness School. Hagerman assented; by 1977, sixteen 'day girls' were attending classes and had also begun to integrate into other aspects of school life.[238] Well aware that full coeducation might be a real possibility for the school, and that it required adequate planning and preparation, the trustees and Hagerman discussed the possibility of accepting female boarders as early as 1970. In the end, however, this momentous step would not be taken until Hagerman's successor came to the school.

Holderness students during Proctor Weekend, circa 1965

Hagerman and the board came together in 1971 to make a different strategic decision for the future of the school. Recognizing the ongoing financial pressures endured by the school—particularly during an era when economics were turbulent on a national scale—they "committed themselves to the nearly impossible task of raising $3,500,000 in a centennial campaign."[239] Though he retired shortly before the school's centennial anniversary in 1979, Hagerman's hard work and vision of financial security for the school had set the stage for the campaign's impressive success. Aside from the monetary achievement, the campaign had made explicit the school's need to maintain and increase its endowment in order to safeguard its future, a message that was lost neither on alumni nor on Hagerman's successors.

As with so many headmasters, the list of Hagerman's concrete achievements does not come close to describing his true legacy to the school. Many of his contributions are likely never to be quantified—the excellent faculty members he hired and supported, for example. Many teachers had a strong personal commitment to Hagerman, and showed their allegiance by performing to a high standard and remaining at the school for long and dedicated tenures. Faculty member Edward Cayley touched on this when describing his first interview at the school. After Cayley had waited over two hours for a late Hagerman, the headmaster and his wife arrived: "Thirty seconds after Don and Ibba finally appeared, [my] considerable annoyance had evaporated in the wind and [I] was their man for life—a perfect example of the effect Don and Ibba have on those around them."[240]

Though it cannot be measured, the warmth and charisma that Hagerman exuded was perhaps his greatest legacy. Not only did it help him to build an extraordinary team of committed faculty and staff members, it also helped him to preserve a feeling of family in the rapidly developing school. And in fact, Hagerman's warmth was his defining characteristic, noted with approval by Weld during Hagerman's first visit to Holderness School. As Weld put it, the new head "drove over to meet the faculty, be introduced to the boys, and captivate all hearts immediately."[241] Hagerman's first impression was a lasting one, and he is remembered as much for his personality as for his achievements.

1977–2001: REV. BRINTON W. WOODWARD, JR.

Holderness School began a significant period of transition when Hagerman retired; his twenty-six year headmastership had been longer than all other headmaster's tenures with the exception of Lorin Webster. The trustees needed to identify a successor who was qualified to carry the school into its second century. Rev. Brinton W. ("Pete") Woodward, Jr. came from the Kent School, where he was the Chaplain, coached three sports, supervised a dorm, and ran the community service program.[242] In addition to his impressive academic credentials and experience, he brought knowledge of other diverse interests, ranging from basketball (he was a Jayhawk at University of Kansas) to volunteer firefighting to acting as a group counselor at a psychiatric center.[243]

Woodward was an able successor, building on many of Hagerman's programs and strengths. The centennial campaign continued to accrue funds as the school's hundredth anniversary approached, and the announcement of its successful completion was an integral part of the 1979 centennial celebrations.[244] Woodward continued efforts to build up the school's funds throughout his tenure, and through various campaigns the endowment rose from around $1.5 million in 1977 to over $24 million in 2000.[245]

The endowment proved to be crucially important to the financial well-being of the school. As its holdings increased, it finally provided the school with the tools to achieve fiscal responsibility. During each of Woodward's twenty-four years, the budget stayed in the black. More importantly, financial aid to students more than doubled during his tenure.[246] The school had weathered the worst of its historic financial difficulties. By reasserting affordable tuition as an institutional priority, it had affirmed the value of the school's founding principles.

The school centennial was celebrated with other projects that also resonated with earlier Hagerman initiatives. The Bioshelter, like the Backward Bound cabin, was funded by an outside grant and combined the construction of a new campus building with academic opportunities.[247] Also known as the Center for Environmental Education, the Bioshelter was a "green" structure intended not only for faculty housing, but also as a teaching tool:

> The energy-efficient features of the bioshelter have become more than theory to the many bioshelter crew (an afternoon sport) members, earth science, and ecology students who have helped to build the Center. [...] They dug, placed forms, shoveled sand and gravel, mixed and tamped grout, pounded nails, measured and cut joints for the raising of a post-and-beam frame, applied insulation, constructed windows, and generally learned what goes into a house from the ground up. The bioshelter, or Center for Environmental Education, will now become a learning space where seminars and research projects on energy and environmental issues are conducted.[248]

Just as students had used the Backward Bound program to learn about local history, they now engaged in the Bioshelter program to learn about environmental issues.[249]

All-school wood gathering for winter at the Bioshelter, 1978

Over time, Woodward also extended the existing Out Back program into a series of non-traditional learning opportunities, which are now known as the Special Programs. The Out Back program remained unchanged, but opportunities in other areas were added one by one. By the mid-1990s, each class spent ten days in March pushing their comfort zones in a particular area. Freshmen and new students explored creativity during Artward Bound, sophomores learned about the importance of service during Habitat for Humanity, juniors faced challenging outdoor experiences on Out Back, and seniors experienced the rigors of college-level academics during Senior Colloquium. Under Woodward, the non-traditional March program begun by Hagerman grew into one of the defining experiences of Holderness School.

Although Woodward was committed to maintaining direction on many Holderness School programs, the school had entered his tenure facing significant decisions on several key issues. At Woodward's first official board meeting, the trustees asked for his reaction on an important matter: a new master plan for campus development. The plan noted that, in the past, the school had deferred "major physical plant expenditures" in favor of a focus on curriculum and faculty. Now, it noted, the campus buildings were increasingly in need of attention:

> [The] normal aging of physical plant and the putting off of certain necessary expenditures has resulted in a backlog of 'must do' situations. New code requirements, upgraded minimum educational standards, consideration of more efficient utility distribution and energy conservation will undoubtedly have to be considered in the near future as necessary items to deal with.[250]

The plan also noted that coeducation was among the future decisions facing the school. Should the school decide to go coed, the building plan would necessarily need to reflect that decision, as the "consultants feel that girls' locker space, upgrading of some sort of girls' lounge, dormitories, and the upgrading of the art, music and drama program would be necessary to accommodate co-education."[251]

The integration of boarding girls was an idea that the trustees had been considering for some time without reaching consensus. As the new headmaster, Woodward had intended to spend his first year evaluating the needs of the school before recommending significant changes, included those related to coeducation. However, Woodward felt that he could not evaluate the building plan effectively without knowing if coeducation would be a factor. With campus development hanging on the decision, the trustees asked Woodward to prepare a recommendation on coeducation.[252]

Within a month, Woodward presented a strategy for fully integrating girls with campus life, and the trustees voted to implement boarding coeducation.[253] Plant development went forward, integrating the needs of female students with those of the rest of the school. The decision to "[implement] our building needs and coeducation needs simultaneously" was in conscious recognition that coeducation brought with it a responsibility to provide equal facilities for boys and girls.[254]

While the board moved ahead with coeducation, Woodward also endorsed an increased presence of minority students at the school. There was only one student of color enrolled at the school in Woodward's first year, and the issue of diversity was extremely important to the new headmaster: he later described it as "a primary reason I went into independent education."[255] In the same year that the school opened its doors to boarding girls, the admissions team undertook new efforts in this direction:

> Minority recruiting has produced at this point four applications from New York City and three from Boston. Most of these boys have been to Holderness School for visits including an overnight stay. We are also pursuing leads to foreign students in hopes that we might bring to the campus a different way of life. It has been very exciting.[256]

The school continued to embrace new strategies for enrolling minority students, including forging partnerships with external recruiting organizations and appealing to parents for help in identifying likely candidates.[257] Woodward's own efforts involved supporting the admissions team in their efforts, meeting with strategists in the field (such as Jesse Jackson), and hiring more faculty members of color.[258] Although it was often a challenge to attract minority and foreign students to the small, rural New England school, successes did come. By the time Woodward left Holderness School, such students comprised almost 10% of total enrollment.[259]

Early in his tenure, Woodward also turned his attention to the role of spirituality on campus. An ordained minister, Woodward deeply valued the important relationship between the school and the Episcopal Church, which had diminished somewhat during the 1960s and 1970s. In fact, during the headmaster search process Woodward had stated clearly to the trustees that "If it's not going to be an Episcopal Church school, I don't want to come."[260] He began the process of reviving the relationship, experiencing some resistance from both faculty and students.[261] However, by the spring of his first year, he informed the trustees that the "storm created by instituting chapel twice a week seems to have abated.

[...] I do not feel that chapel is under particular assault. Many of the services are filled with great singing and positive response."[262] It soon became natural again for the community to come together in the chapel in times of peace and in crisis.[263]

In his second year, Woodward continued the process by adding a theology course requirement back into the curriculum.[264] The concepts of spirituality and service were increasingly incorporated into other aspects of school life as well. An active student Service Committee quickly sprang up, working with a number of community groups on projects such as planting trees, coaching youth soccer clinics, or running fund-raising events for charity.[265] Students participated in Habitat for Humanity beginning in March of 1990.[266] This final addition to the Special Programs underscored the fact that Holderness School valued spiritual development equally with the athletic, academic, and creative development of its students. In 1992, the trustees and faculty took a further step toward acknowledging this fact, and made community service a requirement for graduation.[267]

Woodward's commitment to developing a caring attitude at the school extended beyond his students. He also hoped to base faculty and administrative decisions on a genuine compassion for student needs. To accomplish this, he advocated a balance between discipline and understanding:

> It is my belief and hope that Holderness is both a redemptive community and a community of judgment. It is redemptive in that we try to give the students a sense of worth or self-esteem. [This] comes from feeling important and known to others, from a sense of achievement, from a sense of learning and progress, and from a sense of knowing one's self and his or her strengths and weaknesses. [...] However we must also be a community of judgment. We are not here just to reaffirm individuals as they are, but to help them be more than what they are or think they can be. Therefore, it is important that we tell them when they are wrong, when they have used poor judgment, when they can work harder or do better, and when they have not set their goals high enough.[268]

This approach, commonly referred to as one of "reason and persuasion," became a defining characteristic of the Woodward years at Holderness School.

The methodology was especially important in handling issues related to substance abuse. While the school maintained a policy of expulsion for the use of hard drugs, a student caught with alcohol or marijuana was now often afforded a second chance "coupled with substance abuse evaluation, testing, and possible extended counseling."[269] In 1987, a group of faculty and students began investigating non-disciplinary alternatives for dealing with substance abuse.[270] Their research eventually resulted in what is now known as the CARE team, a group of faculty members who "share information but are dedicated to maintaining confidentiality."[271] By acknowledging that possession of banned substances is often linked to medical or addiction issues, the school reached out to students who needed help but had been afraid of disciplinary consequences.[272]

Woodward walked the walk by remaining closely involved in day-to-day school life. He taught theology throughout his time as headmaster, splitting the course offerings with the school's Chaplain.[273] He reinstated a basketball program at Holderness School (the first practices had to be held in a local gym, where the hoops were attached to the wall and you could slam into the brick "if you were going in for a lay-up and not paying attention").[274] He participated gamely in on-campus activities such as school plays; in one memorable instance, he appeared in royal regalia playing a character referred to as "His Immensity, King Bungle."[275] His strong presence on the campus reinforced the sense that the school was first and foremost a caring community.

Perhaps this involvement is what makes Woodward's strategic skills so impressive. Like his predecessors, he faced enormous responsibilities on campus, but simultaneously remained committed to identifying and pursuing long-range goals that would insure the excellence of the school. During his twenty-four years as headmaster, Woodward was involved in the development of a master plan for the physical plant, two NEAS school evaluations, and several internal long-range plans. When he made the decision to retire, that also was a choice made for the good of the school:

> I am retiring because it is right for the School and right for me. It is right for the School because a transition of the head should be made when a school is strong throughout, such as Holderness is now. A head of school should not stay so long so that he or she departs tired and spiritless and unproductive. A head *should* retire, however, if he or she feels that most or all of his or her goals have been achieved, which is true for me, and which leads me to suspect that the next set of goals should be charted by someone in a position to follow through more thoroughly on them.[276]

Woodward certainly was leaving the school in a position of strength. The endowment was significant, and the school's debt was retired. The physical plant had smoothly incorporated the construction of a slew of new buildings (girls' dormitories, Hagerman Science Center, Alfond Library, Gallop Athletic Center, and a hockey rink), while extensive renovations had improved existing dormitories, as well as the Carpenter and Schoolhouse buildings. However, these remarkable achievements were nevertheless overshadowed by Woodward's accomplishments in less quantifiable areas. As the Chairman of the Board of Trustees noted:

> Pete's greatest accomplishment [...] has been as a leader of people. Over the years he has attracted a group of professionals to our faculty and support staff who are second to none in their talents as educators and role models. [...] All of us—students, faculty, staff, alumni, and trustees—have benefited from Pete's unending devotion, compassion, intellect, work ethic, and sense of fairness.[277]

During Hagerman's time, thoughtful growth had permitted the school to preserve a family culture even while increasing notably in size. Woodward, in a similar manner, maintained the school's focus on people and programs while expanding the physical campus enormously. Perhaps his ability to find a balance between the institutional and the personal, the judicial and the compassionate, was what made Woodward a headmaster in the true Holderness School tradition.

Campus Culture

WOMEN AT HOLDERNESS SCHOOL

Wives and Partners

For the first 100 years of its existence, the school on the old Livermore estate was known as the Holderness School for Boys. However, women and girls always played a role in shaping school culture. Though the forms of women's involvement evolved over the years, the feminine influence was never entirely absent at the school.

While we have only limited knowledge of some aspects of early school life, we do know that the wife of first headmaster Gray played a motherly role to the students. Mrs. Gray was a friendly figure to whom the boys turned when they needed a picnic lunch or other home-like comfort.[278] Headmaster Gray also welcomed and encouraged interaction between the students at Holderness School and the members of the Balch family. Gray tutored the daughters of Mrs. Balch, and the Balch family maintained a warm relationship with the school.[279] As Gray's daughter later recalled:

> The school was very fortunate in having live opposite the widow and children of Canon Balch, most charming and delightful daughters and sons, who were hospitable to an extreme, a tremendous asset to the school life.[280]

Mrs. Balch hosted numerous teas, dinners, and parties for students in her home, and well into the 1900s, her daughters would continue to host students for Sunday teas and other social gatherings.[281]

Many of these social traditions would be embraced as standard duties by the wives of subsequent headmasters. Jennie Adams Webster, for example, was extremely active in school life. Mrs. Webster invited sections of the dormitory over for teas and entertainments during the academic year[282], and also arranged holiday meals and celebrations for those unable to travel home during vacations. Students felt that Mrs. Webster's gatherings provided "a tie between us and home," and had great affection for her because of her efforts.[283] This is clear from their 1905 dedication of the school magazine to her:

> We have all come to realize that Mrs. Webster's devotion to the interests of the school as a whole, and to the happiness and welfare of each individual boy, is so wholesouled and complete as to be a principal feature of that power which the school seeks to wield. What boy will not carry away from his school days most pleasant and grateful memories of the Sunday evening readings with which Mrs. Webster delighted his first-form days? Or who will not remember with equal pleasure her thoughtful and skilful provisions for the long evenings during short vacations? Nor does she seek the happiness of the boys alone. Masters as well will not forget her courtesy and kindness to them on many occasions.
>
> Both Masters and boys must feel that to have known Mrs. Webster and to have had her friendship and kindly interest so freely extended to them is one of the rare privileges of the life here. Out of the fullness of her warm affection for the boys of the school, her earnest desire to cooperate with the Rector and his staff so far as she may, her unselfish devotion to the aims of the school, Mrs. Webster has given us of her best. She has made us happier, but more that that, she has made us better by the power which lofty Christian womanhood must ever exert over boys and men.[284]

Mrs. Webster was equally engaged in activities outside of the school. She was involved with multiple women's societies, including the New Hampshire Federation of Women's Clubs, the Daughters of the American Revolution, and the New Hampshire Women's Auxiliary. Mrs. Webster was not merely a member of these clubs, but an active leader and participant. She was frequently an elected officer[285], and on at least two occasions, she traveled to Washington as a representative of the DAR.[286] The school seemed to take pride in Mrs. Webster's achievements, reporting her activities in the school magazine and remarking upon those occasions when she received visits from notable women.

During headmaster Marshall's time, his mother joined him on campus and would have been the arbiter of school hospitality, as Marshall was unmarried. We know little about the personality of Mrs. Marshall, or indeed about the wives of headmasters Coolbaugh and Richey. This is due in part to the relatively short tenures of their husbands, as well as to a dearth of records for those time periods. Those school records that we do have, however, indicate that these women continued to fill motherly and sisterly roles, providing warmth and friendly advice to students in need.

The school had begun to recognize the importance of women's roles on campus; in fact, the school touted the benefits of their presence in order to convey the image of a home-like campus. By the late 1920s, the school catalog included a statement that "[t]he Rector and his wife are intimate with all the students and are as sincerely interested in them as in their own children."[287] A school view book from this same period featured an image of students at tea with the wife of the headmaster. "The homes of all the Masters are open to each Boy," read the caption. "He is hospitably received and entertained, being trained in conventions and manners through a pleasant social intercourse with ladies and gentlemen."[288] Appropriate interaction with women was seen as an important part of each student's education.

With the rebuilding of campus in 1931, the school finally had accommodations for married faculty members. This meant that there were several more women present on campus, in addition to the wife of the headmaster. Under the guidance of headmaster Weld's wife, Gertrude Mackey Weld, faculty wives began to make more organized contributions to school life. Their focus still frequently centered on the social instruction of students. For example, faculty wives provided the boys with dance lessons[289], and Mrs. Weld continued to host students at gatherings in her home.[290] She also held regular four o'clock Sunday teas for faculty wives and students.[291]

Under Elizabeth ("Ibba") Eames Hagerman, discussions at these teas touched on how faculty wives might help with campus improvements or in other areas. Some of the projects undertaken by the faculty wives included hand-knit sweaters for the ski team and pinch-pleat curtains for newly-built Rathbun dorm.[292] Mrs. Hagerman herself became integral to the development of the school's physical plant:

> [Ibba's] sense of style helped direct the design of campus, and she was largely responsible for the burying of campus power lines, the "variation on a theme" design of the south campus dormitories, and in choosing the architect for the Head's House.[293]

Neither was the more traditional mothering role neglected by Mrs. Hagerman. She was a familiar presence at campus activities, attending every possible home game and serving punch and cookies to the teams on Saturdays. Former students recall that she "always had a kind word to share and knew how to make one feel at home at Holderness."[294]

As the Hagerman era drew to a close, so too did the more traditional roles of wives on the Holderness School campus. For several years, the line between unacknowledged partners and recognized contributors had been blurring. An increasing number of Holderness women were joining the ranks of the school's faculty and staff, and being recognized as such.

Faculty and Staff

Maggie Grennan presides over milk and cookies, circa 1940

The very first female employees of the school were the women who acted as house mothers (also referred to as 'matrons' or 'housekeepers'), laundresses, or as kitchen support. These female staff members were present from the very first years, and were integral to the workings of the school. Though we know little about their specific duties, it is clear from early journals that the boys interacted with them on a daily basis and relied on them for food, laundry, and other domestic support.

By the early 1900s, women were also being brought into the school to fill other roles. Webster hired a woman as his secretary in 1912,[295] as well as a female dance instructor in 1914.[296] Female staff members, like the wives of the headmasters, also provided motherly comfort. When an outbreak of scarlet fever hit campus in 1913, for example, students noted that housekeeper Alice Vason "was especially considerate, going to all sorts of trouble for the benefit of the sick fellows."[297]

By the 1930s and 1940s, women were beginning to fill more than the traditionally female roles of house mother, nurse, secretary, and librarian and were joining the school faculty. These women were frequently (though not always) wives of male faculty members, and taught courses as various as fine arts[298], horsemanship[299], metalworking[300], foreign language[301], and remedial reading.[302] Like the rest of the nation, the school relied heavily upon women's contributions during World War II. However, as a boys' school, Holderness School continued to emphasize the strong male role models that it provided for its students. For many years, the yearbook listed women members of the faculty after the men as "special instructors" (indeed, women's pictures were not included until 1947). This practice gradually fell away, and by the mid-1960s the women on the faculty and staff were represented alongside their male counterparts.

Though there was a gradual change to the number of women on the faculty and staff during these decades, the role of the traditional 'faculty wife' persisted. In fact, most of the female faculty and staff were first and foremost faculty wives who were also interested in taking on additional responsibilities. The idea that a woman might be attracted to pursuing her own career was not yet common at Holderness School. When the wife of a 1956 faculty member took a teaching job at a local school, it was notable enough to be reported in the school's newsletter.[303]

Changing national sentiments continued to affect the role of women at the school. As the women's movement began to make an impact across the country, the number of Holderness School women in the workplace also increased. However, even after the school adopted coeducation, the faculty was still primarily made up of men. This was cause for concern to some:

> [...] I can look around and there are not very many female faculty here. And I think that that's the next step that this institution has to take in order to really become coed. Because I think that as long as you have a male dominated faculty [...] you have girls going to a boys' school, as opposed to a coed institution. And I really think that we need to have role models for girls and you need to have female role models for girls.[304]

The school made a concerted effort to hire more women faculty, though there were some hurdles standing in the way of rapid progress. A woman faculty member pointed out that "it's very awkward to hire a woman, a single woman who will stay or a married woman whose husband is willing to be an appendage, and you can't just always count on [there] being jobs for a couple."[305] Nevertheless, the school persisted in its efforts, gradually improving the gender parity at the school over the ensuing decades. While the employment of full-time women at Holderness School has increased to more equitable numbers, the administration continues to keep the issue in focus as a strategic priority for the school.

Considering Coeducation

Coeducation at Holderness School did not officially come about until the 1978–1979 academic year. That date is somewhat misleading, however. The history of female students at the school is a long one, and the path to coeducation was laid long before the first girls moved into South Campus dormitories.

As was mentioned earlier, headmaster Gray tutored the daughters of the Balch family back in the days of the school's founding.[306] Although the Balch girls did not attend school classes, it could be argued that they were some of the first to receive a Holderness School education. However, the first girl to attend classes with male students was Lorraine Webster (later Mrs. William Starr), the daughter of headmaster Webster and his remarkably dynamic wife. Born in 1887, Starr attended Holderness School for two years before finishing high school at St. Mary's School in Concord. She received her undergraduate degree from Vassar, studied at Boston's Museum of Fine Arts, and became a prominent miniaturist of the day.[307]

Starr's progression from Holderness School to St. Mary's School highlighted the close relationship between the two high schools. Like Holderness School, St. Mary's School was founded by Niles, Coit, and the Episcopal Diocesan Convention. In fact, the school's 1886 opening was based on a mandate to create "a Girls' School of high order [...] where a thoroughly good education shall be given at no greater charge than is now required for boys at Holderness."[308] St. Mary's School survived difficult times that closed other Episcopal girls' schools, and by 1907 had both enlarged and freed itself from debt.[309] Looking to expand, the school moved to Littleton in the 1935–1936 academic year, where it was reborn as St. Mary's-in-the-Mountains.[310]

Through these changes St. Mary's remained a true sister school to Holderness School, and embraced many similar traditions (mountain climbing, skiing, and Gilbert and Sullivan operettas, to name a few).[311] As early as the 1920s, girls from St. Mary's were staples at Holderness School house parties and dances, joining girls from the Plymouth Normal School and Plymouth High School. Holderness School boys returned the favor, traveling to Concord—and later to Littleton—to attend festivities at St. Mary's. This happy relationship continued right through the 1940s, 1950s, and 1960s—and when the 1970s approached, the schools contemplated the benefits of a possible merger.

Holderness School was not on the cutting edge of the coeducation movement. On the contrary, it was relatively conservative in its approach. In the 1969–1970 academic year, the school enrolled faculty daughter Hannah Roberts—the first female day student since Lorin Webster's daughter had attended.[312] However, the trustees were emphatic that Roberts' enrollment was "not to be regarded as the establishment of a policy."[313] This was extraordinarily cautious, given the strong push throughout the independent school community to embrace coeducation.

Hannah Roberts is the first female graduate of Holderness School, 1971

During this time, many independent schools were struggling to meet enrollment quotas, and were simultaneously feeling pressure to open their doors to children of both sexes. This option could be pursued in one of two ways. Coeducation involved teaching boys and girls at a single institution; the National Association of Independent Schools (NAIS) reported that the percentage of coed member schools rose from 38.3% to 66.4% between 1964 and 1974.[314] An alternative to coeducation was coordinate education, which described the choice of two schools to maintain separate identities, but to join together for various classes, sports, and activities. Between 1970 and 1974, seventy-three NAIS member schools merged via the coordinate education route.[315]

By contrast, Holderness School remained wary. Although a few more 'day girls' were admitted in the year following Roberts' enrollment, the trustees limited applications to daughters of faculty and staff.[316] In 1971, they reversed this policy and allowed girls from outside the school community to apply, after being assured that doing so "would not adversely affect the number of boys who could be admitted."[317] The number of day girls slowly grew, reaching fourteen by 1976–1977.[318]

In the meanwhile, the trustees of St. Mary's-in-the-Mountains had proposed the possibility of coordinate education with Holderness School.[319] St. Mary's was experiencing a period of administrative turmoil, and the Holderness School trustees agreed that Hagerman could act as dual headmaster to St. Mary's and Holderness School while they considered the proposal.[320] For the next year, the two schools experimented with combined activities such as concerts, hikes[321], chapel seminars[322], and even some alumni events.[323] In the end, however, the trustees decided that "geographical factors make it unfeasible to operate St. Mary's and Holderness as coordinate schools."[324] The two schools ended the experiment amicably at the end of the 1970–1971 academic year. Soon afterward, St. Mary's made the decision to reduce interactions with Holderness School and instead embrace coeducation.[325] The school is known today as the White Mountain School.

With the option of coordinate education effectively dismissed, the Holderness School trustees turned their attention more fully to the possibility of coeducation. However, they moved guardedly. The trustees' committee on coeducation amassed available research (scant though it was), gathered testimonials from brother and sister schools, and carefully monitored the effect of the growing number of day girls on school life.

A modern eye might view some of the coeducation research of this period with distrust. The arguments of the day tended to cast the debate in terms of the benefit to boys. A 1970 NAIS mailing included research suggesting that the "civilizing influence" of girls and women was one benefit of coeducation; a drawback was that coeducation withdrew limited resources from males, who were counted on to "provide future leadership for [the] community."[326] Certainly more valid considerations were discussed as well, but such concerns highlight the male-centered perspective that was common during this period of social change. Indeed, some of the most vigorous arguments against coeducation came from girls' schools. These educators feared that girls were better served by single-sex schools, where they could speak freely and their education would not be subordinate to that of male counterparts.

From this perspective, Holderness School should be commended, as its trustees preferred to postpone full coeducation rather than treat girl boarders as less than equals. Though some trustees were still unconvinced that coeducation was a wise move for the school, even the proponents of coeducation preferred to delay its implementation until boarding girls could receive appropriate facilities and support.

Equal facilities and support were not enjoyed by the first day girls, though the girls were successfully integrating into the community. Although some girls were made uncomfortable by the tendency of some faculty members to call on them for "a feminine opinion," the girls generally excelled in classes and quickly began amassing academic honors.[327] Faculty members from the time recall that the girls were an exceptional group, perhaps because the school appealed to "a very strong, very self-motivated, very secure girl with lots of energy."[328] The day girls were committed to engaging in every aspect of school life, and got involved with extra-curricular activities wherever possible—choir, drama, yearbook, and other areas in which they could participate.[329]

However, opportunities for the girls were somewhat limited. One young female faculty member recalled starting a cheerleading team because there were no other athletic options for the day girls:

> [W]e made our own skirts and bought the sweaters. [...] You could do it with five or six girls. It was really out of place with the times. It was so uncool to be a cheerleader, then. But there was nothing else for them. And the girls that did it were cute and they really had fun. They were a little embarrassed, but they were good sports about it. [...I]t was just when that was the last thing on earth you should be.[330]

Even when there were finally enough day girls to form a competitive athletic team, as one girl noted, "we must either compete on boys' teams or all agree on one team sport."[331] They reached consensus to form the first girls' team at Holderness School in 1974–1975: a soccer team with a single alternate.[332] One factor in choosing soccer was that it made use of existing athletic equipment, unlike a sport new to the school, such as field hockey. Holderness was still a boys' school, and day girls had to make do with facilities that were not designed to accommodate them.

Even steps taken toward improving facilities for the day girls were not always well-considered. When the trustees purchased a trailer for day girls to use as common space, some felt that it was "something special for the girls," but others believed it marked them as second-class citizens.[333] Even a push to create girls' locker space in the gymnasium was not without controversy. Patricia Henderson, the first Advisor to the Day Girls, recalled the disagreements that arose between even the most well-intentioned faculty members:

> I remember one time there was a plan afoot to have twelve lockers for girls somewhere in Bartsch [...]. And I remember I voted against it, and a faculty member came up afterwards and just hissed at me. [He said, 'You're] not for coeducation at all. [...] How could you turn down that chance to have twelve lockers for twelve girls?' And he missed the point entirely. If you limited yourself to twelve lockers for twelve girls, it would be twelve girls until the year 2000. I remember how angry I was at that. It was one of my angriest moments in [life, I think,] because he just did not see the point.[334]

By the 1975–1976 academic year, these kinds of concerns had become more pressing, and the trustees decided to revisit "the coed situation."[335] As Hagerman wound up his tenure, trustees asked headmaster candidates for their thoughts on coeducation. Meanwhile, the committee on coeducation conducted its own research, assessing faculty opinions and estimating the potential upgrades that would be necessary for curriculum and facilities.

In the summer of 1976, the committee submitted a report to the board that critically underscored the lack of accommodations for day girls, stating that "Holderness must either go all the way or withdraw completely."[336] In the fall of 1977, new headmaster Pete Woodward attended his first board meetings, and informed the trustees that he believed it was time to go coed.[337] Within a month he had presented them with the formal plan for transitioning to coeducation over three to four years; included in this plan was the goal of hiring more women faculty as role models.[338] After vigorous debate, the trustees approved the plan by ballot.[339]

In the fall of 1978, twelve boarding girls and thirteen day girls took part in the first 'official' year of coeducation at Holderness School. The transition plan allowed for incremental increases in girls each year, and—like the first day girls—the first girl boarders were spectacular salespeople for coeducation at the school.[340] Fears that programs such as Out Back would suffer were dispelled as the year progressed; as Woodward later said, "Having the boys watch the girls *more* than pull their own weight went a long way toward dispelling misconceptions."[341] Hockey, Alpine skiing, Nordic skiing, tennis, and lacrosse teams were all available to girls in the first year, and more teams were added as the numbers of girls increased.[342]

Perhaps not surprisingly, applications to Holderness School increased by 70% in the first year that coeducation was officially adopted.[343] In the 25 years that have elapsed from that time to this, day girls, new girls, and women faculty have become integral to the Holderness experience. And the Holderness experience seems not to have changed on a fundamental level—the girls who have come to Holderness School have embraced and benefited from the school, while enriching the community with their contributions.

SPIRITUALITY AND SERVICE

Spiritual Roots

Holderness School is, quite literally, the spiritual child of the Episcopal Church in New Hampshire. When Bishop Niles encouraged the Diocesan Convention to plan and build the school in the 1870s, he was the first of a long line of Episcopal bishops to become intimately involved with the school. In fact, the Episcopal Bishop of New Hampshire is, to this day, the ex officio president of the school's Board of Trustees. Because it was an Episcopal institution, the campus life at Holderness School was to be overseen by an ordained headmaster, referred to as the Rector. However, the ties between the school and the church went far beyond these official relationships.

In fact, the school inherited long-standing associations with the Episcopal Church when the trustees accepted Emily Balch's offer of the old Livermore estate. Samuel Livermore's wife, Jane, was the daughter of Rev. Arthur Browne, rector of the first Episcopal Church in New Hampshire ("Queen's Chapel" in Portsmouth, now known as Saint John's Episcopal Church).[344] The Livermores therefore brought to Holderness a strong loyalty to the Episcopal Church, and in fact Jane is credited with converting many of her Puritan neighbors to the religion.[345] The Livermores read Episcopal services with these neighbors in Livermore Mansion until 1797, when they helped to build Trinity Church.[346] This structure was sometimes referred to as "Lady Livermore's Chapel" or "Old Trinity," and was only the second Episcopal Church to be built in New Hampshire.[347]

Chapel on Chocorua Island, circa 1905

Trinity Church, circa 1905

Exterior view of the Chapel of the Holy Cross, circa 1895

Interior view of the Chapel of the Holy Cross at Easter, circa 1895

The Livermore family tutor, Rev. Robert Fowle, was asked to become the town's pastor in 1789, and once Trinity Church was built he performed his services in part from that pulpit.[348] When Fowle passed away in 1847, however, the simple building fell into disuse, and "the church at Plymouth became the chapel of a cemetery."[349] There would be no more regular services at the church until the arrival of the Balch family in the 1860s, when Rev. Balch began serving as rector of Trinity Church.[350]

When the trustees later accepted the offer from Balch's widow to locate Holderness School in the old Livermore Mansion, it was therefore fitting that the opening sermon be given in Trinity Church.[351] In fact, the school's first Rector held services there every Sunday to supplement the weekday services held in the school building, a tradition that continued until the school's own chapel was built in 1884.[352] Though the Chapel of the Holy Cross fills most of the school's needs, school services are still held in Trinity Church at least once a year around Memorial Day. Thus the school not only maintains a relationship with the current Episcopal Diocese, but also by tradition celebrates its ties to the earliest days of the Episcopal Church in New Hampshire.

Community Ties

Perhaps because of its deep-rooted bond to the Episcopal Diocese and Trinity Church, Holderness School has also enjoyed close relationships with other churches in the area. For example, St. Mark's Episcopal Church in Ashland shares ties with the school that go back to its earliest history. Rev. Howard F. Hill, who gave the opening sermon for Holderness School, had acted as pastor of both St. Mark's and Trinity Church.[353] In later years, St. Mark's gained a minister from the ranks of the school when they persuaded the Rev. Lorin Webster, then a teacher at Holderness School, to assume parish duties at St. Mark's. Turnabout is fair play, and in 1892 the school lured Webster back to become its third headmaster.[354] This back-and-forth was not an indication of rivalry, but rather of a close relationship between the institutions. Webster had a loyalty to both places, and was known to preach sermons at St. Mark's during his time as Holderness School headmaster.[355]

In fact, Webster and later headmasters would often travel to other churches to preach, and welcomed visiting pastors to preach at Holderness School's services as well. These spiritual exchanges were only some of the threads that helped connect the school to churches in the state; others were ties of music and service. The choir of the school's Chapel of the Holy Cross frequently traveled throughout New Hampshire, and as early as the 1880s the students were performing as far away as Grace Episcopal Church in Manchester.[356] By 1898 the choir had begun to take part in an annual choir festival, and singing activities took them beyond

St. Mark's and Grace Church to churches in Portsmouth[357], Claremont[358], Concord[359], and other locations throughout the state. It was a tradition that would continue, in one form or another, through at least the 1950s.[360]

Because community membership involves service, members of the school did their part to support religious organizations that were in need. Collections taken during school chapel services were often donated to churches or charities in need of financial support, both within and beyond the state of New Hampshire.[361] During both the 1940s[362] and the 1950s[363], the school hosted the youth conferences for the Episcopal diocese on campus during the summer. When Trinity Church wanted to square its cemetery bounds in 1969, Holderness School donated about a half-acre of school property to the Cemetery Church Yard Association.[364] But students and faculty were always willing to give more hands-on assistance; when the Chapel of the Holy Spirit in Plymouth made its start back in 1924, students helped "prepare the building for use," headmaster Marshall acted as Priest-in-Charge, and faculty member Rev. Leslie Walter Hodder was its curate.[365]

In fact, members of the Holderness faculty were often known to take positions in nearby churches. From the Trinity Church pulpit, first headmaster Frederick Gray served not only his students but also members of the community. Lorin Webster, in addition to his various visiting sermons at nearby churches, for some time held regular services in Plymouth's Universalist Church on alternate Sundays.[366] Leslie Hoddard, who acted as curate at the Chapel of the Holy Spirit, eventually left Holderness School and began a new church in Berlin, New Hampshire (the school donated money to this venture from its own chapel collections, and solicited contributions from alumni and friends as well).[367] As late as 1957, Holderness School Chaplain William Judge acted as another Priest-in-Charge at the Chapel of the Holy Spirit.[368] Whether assuming roles "supplemental to [...] Holderness duties" or accepting permanent positions in other institutions, members of the school's faculty forged and maintained strong ties with the surrounding religious community.[369]

Chapel Services and Sacred Studies

Campus customs have reflected the historical ties between the school and the church in different ways through the years. However, spirituality has always been an underlying pillar of the school, regardless of shifts in forms of observance during certain eras. Certainly there has been a recurring tradition of healthy debate between students and the administration about what religion's role should be in the campus experience.

Early on, of course, students did not question the requirements to attend prayers or their classes in Sacred Studies. These events were part of the daily rhythm of school life. "We went to prayers as usual," writes a student in 1883, "and after that Mr. Gray read the names for bounds [a disciplinary restriction]. I was not among the number, but came near it." Of a typical Sunday, the same student records that he "went to church both forenoon and afternoon, and also to sacred studies in the evening."[370] Students at this time did not appear to take undue notice of the religious aspects of school life. They simply accepted them as conventional, if sometimes inconvenient, incursions on what might otherwise be recreation time.

An inconvenience to be endured: this was probably not so different from how later students (even some current students) would view chapel services. In an article printed in The New Hampshire Churchman, Weld acknowledged the challenges inherent to providing a religious education:

> No head of a Church school deludes himself into thinking that all boys pray when prayers are being said, or that there are not at times boys who have no thanks to offer beyond 'Thank God it's over' at the conclusion of a service. And schoolmasters realize that adolescence, in school and often more markedly in college, is a time when some boys go through periods of feeling responsible for no one but themselves, and the fact that religion is social does not enter their consciences: there's nothing in it for them, no need and no obligation. But it is our hope as we watch boys slip into it, either in or after school, that this stage is only temporary, and that with new responsibilities will come not only a return of the old idealism but also a return of the old habit of saying their prayers, and turning to the Church for strength.[371]

Weld captured Holderness School's philosophy in a nutshell: if you instill in students a familiarity with a religious tradition, they will be better equipped for later life. In other words, awareness of the spiritual aspects of their lives makes it possible for students to turn to the church (any church) for comfort and strength during some future time of need.

Though the school was clear-eyed and practical about students' attitudes, students increasingly pushed the question of the relevance of religious studies to contemporary life. In the 1950s, early rumbles were reflected by student editorials in the school paper. "What are the reasons behind the compulsory chapel rule?" asked one student. "Religion is not a thing someone can hand out on a silver platter. Everyone must work out his own religion for himself."[372] Weld answered such queries clearly in his response to another such editorial. "'Freedom of ignorance' is not one of the fundamental American freedoms," he wrote.

> Schools have considerable latitude and equal responsibility in selecting the knowledge to which they choose to expose American boys and girls during school age. [...] This school has adopted the principle that as exposure to Shakespeare, mathematics, science, history, language, and physical education will probably result in an enrichment of personality, so will exposure to Chapel, prayers, and courses in Sacred Studies.[373]

Nevertheless, the debate only strengthened during the next few decades. The divisiveness of this and other issues on campus was symptomatic of unhappiness at the national level, where a true generation gap appeared to be widening. When headmaster Hagerman arrived, "students were attending chapel three evenings a week, twice on Sunday, and each day began with a hymn and prayers."[374] Hagerman wanted to keep the school true to its traditions, but also relevant to its students. He continued to assert the importance of chapel services, though formal classes in sacred studies began to fall by the wayside around 1957.[375] "Holderness was founded and dedicated to the proposition that there is a power greater than man," he avowed. "Chapel has a place in our daily life."[376]

And chapel services did remain, though the formats and frequency of services would evolve. The headmaster did his best to hear and address the concerns of the students, hoping to minimize the students' perception of the generation gap as best he could. In 1969, he invited Bishop Hall to moderate a well-received forum about the role of chapel services at the school.[377] In 1971, Hagerman acknowledged that "compulsory attendance at chapel cannot assure worship or a student's commitment."[378] Students were soon required to attend only one service per week, and that service could be in the school's chapel, at a Plymouth congregation, or in an approved alternative format (discussion groups, chapel dramas, and chapel concerts, for example). The non-traditional services focused on "religious and ethical implications of direct man to man relationships, and of the place of God in these encounters;" they were meant to foster "the spirit of free inquiry."[379]

By encouraging student involvement in the design of chapel services, and listening to their concerns, Hagerman seemed to have averted a crisis that was very much of its time. As the tensions of the 1960s and 1970s began to ebb, he reinstituted a regular Monday morning chapel service.[380] When headmaster Woodward came to the school in 1977, he immediately supplemented this with a second weekly chapel service, and had a theology course requirement in place by his second year.[381]

Today, religious studies and chapel requirements remain a part of every student's campus experience. However, perhaps as a result of lessons learned during some difficult decades, these experiences are tied not only to the rich Episcopal tradition of the school, but also to the individual experiences of members of the community. Chapel services now regularly incorporate talks by students, faculty members, and guests, a tradition started in 1981 during Woodward's tenure.[382] The school also encourages students to consider spiritual paths that may be revealed to them during their experiences of the outdoors. As Woodward wrote in 2000, "[w]hen we fully embrace nature for all that it is [...] then we embrace and discover God as well."[383] Though some of these approaches feel new, the school's spiritual goal—to expose students to experiences of faith that will serve them well in future—remains unchanged.

Service

A natural outgrowth of the school's religious tradition is its commitment to service. In early years, this manifested itself in the spontaneous generosity of the students and faculty to those around them. There was a simple expectation that, as a part of a community, one individual would help another in times of need, and Holderness School both gave and received such assistance.

The risk of fire, one of the biggest threats to safety in the earlier years of the school, was an area where this give and take is well-illustrated. Forest fires or building fires could rage out of control and swiftly destroy property and take lives, and communities rallied to help each other when threatened.

Many alumni are already aware of at least three occasions when Holderness School was on the receiving end for this sort of assistance. In the spring of 1883, a fire razed the old Livermore Mansion, leaving almost seventy-five people temporarily homeless. "The warmest gratitude is ever due to the people of Plymouth for their generous hospitality and care of the members of the school in their sudden extremity," reflected an author in 1890. "The school enjoyed the kind entertainment of friends for several days."[384] In February of 1931 a fire seriously damaged the east wing of Knowlton Hall, despite the precautions that had been taken with brick construction and fire escapes. The fire was contained by the combined efforts of students and firemen from Plymouth, but the dorm was, temporarily, uninhabitable. Once again, friends from the town of Plymouth came forward and "were exceedingly generous in putting the boys up for the night."[385] This fire was but a foreshadowing of the momentous blaze that overwhelmed the building in October of the same year. Nothing could be done to save the structure this time. When the trustees closed the school for an impromptu ten-day vacation, friends in Plymouth once again provided housing for students arranging for travel home. The Mt. Prospect Lodge provided housing for those students and faculty members who instead opted to stay, and "cheerfully stored and sorted, salvaged and painted."[386]

Fewer people may realize that the generous support provided by the school's neighbors reflected a pattern of assistance offered by the school itself. In fact, since its inception, the school had consistently offered aid and sympathy to those under threat of fire damage. There are accounts of students, with the blessing of the administration, interrupting classes and other activities in order to help to fight local fires in 1889[387], 1904[388], 1927[389], 1930[390] and 1947[391]. The moody Pemigewassett River also provided opportunities to help neighbors. During a flood in 1927, for example, "[t]he boys of the school helped the people, at the foot of the hill, to remove their furniture when the flood reached their houses and also to take it back after the flood subsided."[392]

The impulse to be of service often occurred in spontaneous reaction to immediate community needs. Over time, however, more formalized approaches to service emerged. At times of national or international crisis, students planned fundraising activities and drives. During World War II, for example, two boys organized a clothing drive for a British relief organization called *Young America Wants To Help*, securing 100% participation from the student body.[393] Students also participated in regular charitable activities above and beyond donating to the collection taken during chapel services. Students voted to participate in a weekly "austerity meal" observed throughout the 1940s and 1950s; this saved the school money that was instead applied to community donations like Thanksgiving baskets for local families.[394] Eventually, a variety of volunteer activities were organized under a single student service committee, which had various incarnations during different eras.[395]

Acts of service to the community were mirrored by an internal culture of self-sufficiency and volunteerism at the school. The "self-help" plan, now known as the Jobs Program, was begun by Edric Weld after the 1931 fire, and was modeled on a similar program first tried at the Kent School.[396] Under this program, students assumed responsibility for various tasks of campus upkeep (serving meals, raking leaves, etc.) in order to make the school run more efficiently and cheaply. Though the new program was put in place in part to mitigate the rebuilding costs facing the school, it had other benefits. Because "all boys were to do the same amount, whether scholarship recipients or not," every student soon had a vested interest in the upkeep of the school that he shared equally with every other student.[397] This is an incalculable benefit that has encouraged the school to retain the Jobs Program even to the present time.

The benefit, of course, was not just to the school, but also to the character of Holderness School students. As with sacred studies and chapel services, the experience of volunteerism was seen as a formative one for each graduate. In 1992, the school adopted a new graduation requirement that formally required students to undertake some form of public service during their time at the school. The Dean of Faculty at the time, Jim Nourse, echoed Weld's 1950 defense of religious curricula in his explanation of the decision:

> We believe very strongly that service to others is integral to the mission of the Holderness School. Since service should play an important role in shaping the character of a Holderness student, we think it ought to exist as a fundamental orientation in the day-to-day life of the community. And we like to believe that as a result of that orientation, service will become part of the lifestyle of Holderness alumni as they carry on with their lives.[398]

The new graduation requirement was not intended to add extra commitments to student life, but instead, to recognize and encourage the work that so many students were already doing. In particular, seniors were already frequently using their senior projects to pursue a "service-oriented program," and sophomores were able to spend two weeks with Habitat for Humanity during the spring-term's Special Programs.[399] In many ways, the new graduation requirement simply codified what was already a long-standing school tradition of service and volunteerism.

Holderness Traditions

Indeed, tradition is a word that cannot be avoided when describing Holderness School's religious heritage. In a larger sense, the tradition of the Episcopal Church is at the root of the school's spiritual practices, from the form of the chapel rites to the stimulus toward service. But the religious customs touch almost all aspects of school culture. Surely every graduate recalls a particular chapel service as representing a rite of passage at the school.

The earliest alumni might have reflected on an old All Saints' Day tradition, when, before a special chapel service in Old Trinity could begin, the choir marched around "all the walks" in the cemetery singing hymns.[400] Or perhaps they preferred to recall Easter services in the Chapel of the Holy Cross, when the service was "fully attended" by members of both the community and the school, and the "altar was beautifully decked with flowers and the singing was splendid."[401]

Certainly graduates can recall with pleasure one of the Christmas traditions observed during their time at the school. Perhaps they participated in the party for community children, where each student at the school brought a gift for a child.[402] Possibly they remember a Santa Lucia or Christmas pageant, with faculty children processing down the chapel aisle in festive costume.[403] Surely they have a warm memory of a Candlelight Service, Hanging of the Greens, or Lessons and Carols service in the Chapel of the Holy Cross. These traditions were yearly milestones in school life—not only religious services, but also events that marked the passage of time.

Mrs. Weld consults with Santa Claus, circa 1939

Personal milestones were also passed at the school, with Chaplains and rectors performing all of the weddings, baptisms, ordinations, and memorial services that are associated with religious life. And it may be that it is in these services that we can see the power of the school's philosophy toward religious education. For not only students take part: alumni return to campus, year after year, for such services. A seed of faith—perhaps planted at the school—has taken root and brought them back to celebrate a religious tradition.

Bishop Smith said once that "knowledge without morality is dangerous, and morality without knowledge is ineffectual."[404] For some students, formal church services will never become comfortable. For others, a church congregation may henceforth become a place of refuge in times of distress. Regardless, Holderness School continues the struggle to awaken its students to the moral questions that face them daily, and to prepare them with an ethical, perhaps spiritual, grounding which will support them throughout their lives.

ACADEMICS

Preparing Students For Success

At Holderness School, changes to curricula have reflected adjustments to the school's placement goals for graduating seniors. The school began in the post-Civil War years, and many of its first students came from military families.[405] At the time, the school advertised that its students could be "fitted for College, the United States Naval and Military Academies at Annapolis and West Point, and the higher Scientific Schools."[406] These placement goals were reflected in the academic structure that was in place by 1885, which encouraged students to choose from one of four formalized tracks:

1. Classical Course. This course is arranged for four years; and contains the studies required for admission to College. The subjects of study are Latin, Greek, Algebra, Plane Geometry, Greek and Roman History, Ancient Geography, French, selected English and American authors, and English Composition.

2. Scientific Course. The Scientific Course is arranged for three years; and contains the requirements for admission to the higher Scientific Schools and Schools of Technology, including the United States Naval and Military Academies at Annapolis and West Point. The subjects of study are Arithmetic, Algebra, Plane, Solid and Spherical Geometry, Trigonometry and Mensuration; and their applications to Navigation and Surveying, Geography, Ancient and. Modern History, French or German, Chemistry, Physics, Botany and Physiology.

3. Commercial Course. The studies of this course are Arithmetic, Algebra, Book-keeping, Commercial Law, Constitution of the United States,

Ancient and Modern History, and French or German, arranged for three years.

4.   English Course. This course is arranged for four years, and consists of Arithmetic, Algebra, Geometry, Descriptive and Physical Geography, Ancient and Modern History, Hygiene and Physiology, Chemistry, Physics, Botany, Drawing, English Grammar, and the critical reading and study of Standard Authors.[407]

It is unclear how many students were interested in each course in the earliest years. In the years between 1885 and 1892, however, the most popular option was the Classical Course. While interest in the English and Scientific Courses waxed and waned without a discernible pattern, a steady—if small—stream of Holderness School students enrolled in the Commercial Course and prepared themselves for working life.

When headmaster Lorin Webster arrived in 1892, he changed the format of the curriculum somewhat. The school catalog published in his first year no longer mentioned preparation for military academies, nor did it refer to a student cadet corps. This is notable, because only a year before the cadet corps' "instruction in military tactics" had been touted as "an integral part of the physical training which the boys receive."[408] The changes under Webster perhaps reflected a larger shift of focus away from the Civil War.

The academic program also changed. It was now divided into five "grades" that offered studies linked to the tracked Courses; presumably, this made it easier to accept new students of different ages.[409] The school still prepared its boys for "admission to the leading colleges and scientific schools," but the school catalog warned that "unless a boy has a decided talent for Mathematics and the Natural Sciences, the regular Classical Course is recommended."[410] At the same time, every student was now allowed, "under proper advice," to choose coursework "with particular reference to his chosen college or scientific school."[411] College counseling had been born, and individual placement goals for students were beginning to become explicit.

Admissions policies were also made more rigorous under Webster. Immediately previous to his tenure, the catalog described entrance qualifications as follows:

Boys are received at the school at any age over ten years, and can enter at any part of the course for which they may be found qualified. There are no literary requirements for admission, excepting ability to read and write; but each applicant must present satisfactory testimonials of good moral character.[412]

By the next year, requirements had changed:

> An applicant for admission to the First Grade should be twelve years of age and should be able to pass an examination in the studies generally taught in the public schools of the Grammar grade. Candidates for the higher grades will be expected to pass a satisfactory examination in the studies already pursued in the respective grades.[413]

As the adoption of entrance exams illustrates, there was at this time a growing recognition of the need to standardize the curriculum for each grade level.

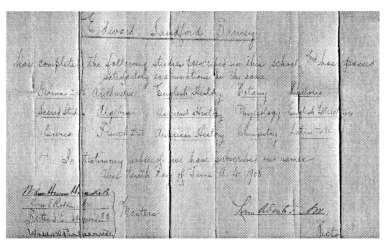

Detail from the diploma of Edward Sandford Barney, 1908.

It took several years for Holderness School to apply the principle to its own academics. In the fall term of 1908, however, the school transformed the coursework and evaluation for each grade (now referred to as "forms"[414]) so that they might be "brought into agreement with those adopted by the College Examining Board, accepted by the Carnegie Foundation, and generally used in the foremost schools in this country."[415] The curriculum for first formers was in essence a final year of elementary coursework, but students in the second form entered one of three new study tracks. These were rearrangements of the former courses, designed to prepare students for specific collegiate goals. Curriculum tracks I and II were intended to prepare students for pursuit of an A.B. college degree (the former to include Greek studies, and the latter not). The third track was for students interested in either a B.S. degree or a career in technology.[416]

The implications of this change in curriculum were monumental. By bringing its academics in line with standards defined by an outside organization, Holderness School had identified its place in a larger community of educational institutions. Each year, small adjustments continued to result from this shift in perspective. In 1911, the school began to recognize "certificates from schools of good repute," and waived entrance exams for prospective students bearing those certificates.[417] Qualifications for receiving a Holderness School diploma were made explicit in 1915: at that time, each student needed a 70% average to graduate, and an 80% average to be recommended for college entrance[418] (the diploma was later also made contingent upon the number of class units completed by the student).[419]

Clarifying the graduation requirements made it easier for other schools to assess the quality of Holderness School graduates. The benefits of this type of transparency were to come quickly. In the 1918 catalog, the school proudly announced that "Holderness boys are admitted to Trinity, and Dartmouth Colleges, without examination, on the School's certificate."[420] Holderness School later made the same arrangement with Cornell University,[421] Worcester Polytechnic Institute,[422] and all "colleges represented on the New England College Entrance Certificate Board."[423]

When headmaster Alban Richey came to Holderness School in 1929, he abandoned the three formal curriculum tracks set up during Webster's time. Instead of providing separate arcs of coursework to span multiple years of study, Richey reverted to having one standard course of study assigned to each form.[424] The exception was the curriculum for the new sixth form, where students might have individualized coursework composed of "selections made according to the requirements of the college the student expects to enter."[425]

This structure changed yet again when Richey was succeeded by Edric Weld a few years later. Focusing on the academics for the students of high school age, Weld outlined two courses of study: a College Preparatory Course, and a General Course "designed especially for those who have difficulty with foreign languages or who for other reasons do not plan to enter college."[426] Students pursuing either of these courses of study chose from the same pool of classes, but mixed them in different proportions to attain the appropriate academic credits for their goals.

By 1946, the notion of codified tracked courses had faded altogether. The catalogs explained that "the course of study which each boy actually takes is worked out on the basis of his previous training, his special interests, and his capacities as indicated by diagnostic tests."[427] Around this time, the catalogs also began listing courses primarily by department rather than by form.[428] This was, in part, an acknowledgement of how difficult it had become to chronologically outline a principal course of study at Holderness School.

Graduation from Holderness School was now contingent upon a student's completion of a given number of full-year courses, with the understanding that some departmental quotas would also be met.[429] The school no longer defined an exact roster of courses based on students' specific college goals, but instead defined students courses of study based on their personal interests and goals. Faculty recommended certain choices as being appropriate for particular situations, and required students to meet certain baseline academic requirements defined by the school. This model has persisted into the present day.

This is not to say that the expectations of colleges and universities went unheeded. Holderness School continued to monitor its course offerings carefully, tailoring them as needed to provide content that would best help its graduates in their future endeavors. One notable result of this process was the introduction of the Advanced Placement course into the school curriculum.

AP preparation was first offered in the late 1970s, when Calculus and French V classes were geared toward their respective AP tests.[430] Similar preparation was gradually added to other courses. By 1983 there were at least six AP options for motivated students,[431] and more continued to be added into the next decades.[432] Holderness School was providing a high number of AP offerings for a relatively small school. In 1997, Dean of Academic Affairs Janice Pedrin-Nielson explained that the AP selection challenged students and diversified course offerings; in addition, she noted, "we want colleges to have the external measures that these courses—and our AP test scores—provide in understanding out whole curriculum better, and its rigor in relation to other schools."[433] The inclusion of AP courses gave choice to students, but also clarified the value of a Holderness School education.

As colleges began to diversify, the school had a growing need to ensure that students made smart choices about where to pursue that education. In 1960, Holderness School joined the Association of College Admissions Counselors, a move that extended its college placement horizons from the Northeast to the Midwest.[434] Colleges and universities had been visiting the Holderness School campus since the 1950s, meeting prospective applicants and describing their own educational goals. Holderness School continued to build relationships with these schools, hoping to be better equipped to find good matches for its graduates. In 1985, Holderness School hosted its first College Night, attended by over forty colleges as well as by some other local high schools.[435] The goal for the evening was "to put more of our students in contact with more of the colleges' representatives."[436]

This tradition continued into the 1990s. Today, however, Holderness School students meet individually at the school with representatives of colleges and universities. These visits are coordinated through the school's Office of College Counseling, which now takes responsibility for helping students match with appropriate colleges or universities. The OCC recognizes that every student has different needs, and that these needs cannot be met by every school:

> For Holderness, a good match means: the student will be stretched academically and yet still find success; the student will find and make lasting and meaningful friendships; and the student will be able to actively pursue those extra-curricular interests which they [sic] value.[437]

In its earliest years, Holderness School offered courses that would, its administration believed, provide students with a sound educational footing and opportunities to continue on diverse paths. Military opportunities, in particular, loomed large in this post-Civil War period. As standardization began to sweep through educational institutions, the school began to more closely tailor its curriculum to the expectations of colleges and universities. When it became impracticable to provide tracked curricula to satisfy every college, Holderness School created course offerings that were diverse enough to meet the individual needs of both students and colleges. However, despite the choices open to students, the school today remains focused on ensuring that a Holderness School education, by definition, meets standards of the highest quality.

Outside Influences

Just as the original course of studies at Holderness School was influenced by the ghost of the Civil War, later curriculum was also shaped by national and international events. Whenever an incident or social movement threatened to affect the futures of graduates, the academic goals of the school required adjustment. Sometimes these effects were felt only temporarily, and the school returned to a status quo within a few years. Occasionally, however, reactions to outside developments were more lasting, becoming part of the school's educational philosophy.

On the eve of the First World War, young high school seniors could expect to face increased and sobering responsibilities upon graduation. Webster attended a headmasters' conference in Hartford, Connecticut to discuss the question "How is the Prep school boy going to aid his country in this time of need?"[438] Students, as well as faculty, were well aware of the heavy expectations that were to rest on their shoulders. Articles and editorials in the school magazine reminded them that "boys who have this opportunity [of a Christian education] must be the coming leaders in all times of national perplexity and anxiety."[439]

Schools, therefore, were accountable for preparing students for a new, grim future. The first priority was no longer to place a boy in college, but to groom him for looming adult responsibilities. There were different ways to do this (Webster did discuss the reintroduction of a student military drill[440]), but the preferred approach was to urge students to focus on their academics. A student editorial summed this up by explaining that each student's "steady application to the present duties" would "prepare competent citizens on whose shoulders the burdens of the Republic will one day fall."[441]

During World War II, Edric Weld faced a similar challenge. He was deeply troubled by the war, which he felt was in part a result of "the hollowness of much twentieth century education in both Europe and America."

> We now realize that there is no necessary connection between the accumulation of information in a specific field [...] and the attainment of wisdom [...] Neither is growth in wisdom necessarily accompanied by the habit of acting according to that knowledge. Upon the schools of today lies the responsibility both for mental training and also for providing the background of emotion and habit from which alone we can hope that the peace of the future will depend not on politicians and pressure groups, but upon an informed and purposeful electorate.[442]

Predicting that 50% of his students at this time would never go on to college, Weld believed that schools like Holderness would "be terminal rather than preparatory."[443] He wanted Holderness School to better prepare his students to be citizens of the world, and to provide them with "more of the responsibility and opportunity for initiative which colleges are now supplying rather than schools."[444] To do this, Weld tweaked specific courses (adding material about democracy and social organizations, for example) and increased student responsibility for the direction of extra-curricular activities and other aspects of school life.[445] Even in the years following the war, Weld would retain his belief that college placement was less important than the need to "educate and develop the whole boy in mind, spirit, and body."[446]

In times of peace, prep schools generally reverted to focusing on college placement goals for their graduates. But by the time the Vietnam era rolled around, war was not the only factor diverting students from college. Some students were postponing college—perhaps indefinitely—in favor of work, travel, or other experiences; even college-bound seniors were disengaging from the school during their final spring terms.[447] Many under-form students, in the meanwhile, were agitating for more relevant curricula.

Headmaster Donald Hagerman was sensitive to these concerns. New courses in branches of sociology, ecology, technology, and other issues were added to the curriculum in the late 1960s. As one long-time faculty member described this development, "curriculum evolution over epochs was replaced by instant revolution."[448] But to keep seniors engaged in academic work during their final spring term required a more unusual approach than simple changes to course content.

As early as 1962, the school was allowing some students to focus on an academic project rather than a spring sport during their final years.[449] In 1969, this academic option was formally endowed by Mr. and Mrs. Norman McCulloch Jr. in memory of their son Bill '70. This separate project option for seniors released them from classes during the last month of spring term[450] in order "to pursue special interests not possible in the normal limits of the school curriculum."[451]

Pursue them they did. Though the administration did have to adopt a policy of turning down "numerous unimaginative proposals," the majority of topics were original and inspiring.[452] Many of the projects were service-oriented, and most took full advantage of the unique opportunity of time and funding provided by the endowed program. The number of senior projects fluctuated from year to year, depending on the level of student interest and quality of the proposals. However, the program continued without many changes into the present day. All told, an impressive number of Holderness School graduates have pursued unique experiences all over the world as a result of the program.

The school benefited by Hagerman's willingness to react to student concerns during this time. However, his curriculum changes were not entirely reactive. Hagerman felt, as Weld did in an earlier era, that "emphatic priority should be given to secondary school education as an experience in itself and not solely in preparation for admission for college."[453] This viewpoint would lead Hagerman to support perhaps the most significant modification to date of the Holderness School curriculum: the addition of the unique educational modules known as Special Programs.

Special Programs

Out Back (originally called Outward Bound) was the first of the Special Programs to be implemented at Holderness School. It was begun in 1969, the same year that Senior Projects were endowed. OB, as it is commonly referred to, is currently described on the Holderness School's website as follows:

> After on-campus instruction in safety, first aid, and cold-weather survival techniques, the junior class is divided into small groups, each accompanied by two well-trained faculty leaders. The groups disperse into the surrounding mountains, beginning their journey with a three-day shakedown hike on snowshoes or skis. This is followed by a three-day solo period, during which students are required to write letters to themselves. Letters are sealed by students, and collected by faculty members; they are mailed to their authors two years later. Following the solo period, the Out Back program concludes with a four-day group hike.[454]

Though accurate, this concise description does not perhaps adequately convey the power of the OB experience. The ten-day excursion is often described by alumni as transformative, even as their most important Holderness School memory. It was designed to have just this sort of impact.

In 1969 two faculty members, Bill Clough and Fred Beams, participated in the national Outward Bound program. They emerged believing that Holderness School should offer a similar experience, and that students and faculty would learn from facing challenges together as peers.[455] Hagerman agreed. The first session of OB took place on Dec. 8, 1969 with forty-three students, five Holderness School faculty members, and three leaders from the Dartmouth Outward Bound Center participating.[456]

OB quickly became a staple of the Holderness School experience, and in 1976, the program was endowed through donations from alumni and the DeWitt Wallace Fund, Inc.[457] This endowment allowed the school to offer equipment to everyone participating in the program.[458] A review of the program in 1980 applauded the "keen sense of pride among students, faculty, and administration [toward OB] and a mystique which surrounds the program," but pointed out that inexperienced faculty, lack of training, and minimal emergency capabilities could present future problems.[459] These concerns were taken seriously, and student and faculty training and preparation have been a major feature of the OB program ever since.

Other aspects of the program also changed over the years. The name was changed to protect Outward Bound, Inc.'s copyright; outside instructors were no longer used; excursions were moved to the month of March in order to take advantage of longer daylight hours. However, the core features of the program were preserved, and the experience still challenges participants as effectively as it did back in 1969.

The physical challenges inherent to OB were soon complemented by a program that presented students with a creative challenge. Under new headmaster Pete Woodward, faculty members Jay Stroud and Charlotte Brooks began Artward Bound, or AB, in 1979.[460] In its earliest incarnation, AB was a practical solution to the administrative and academic headaches presented by having so many students away during OB, when it was nearly impossible to continue classroom studies as usual. A typical day in the first years of AB consisted of some academic work in the early morning, followed by formal arts presentations and hands-on work; afternoons included a sports program.[461] At that point, AB utilized the non-OB faculty as AB instructors, teaching their own hobbies or interests.[462]

It was fairly clear that this model was not ideal. The power behind OB was in having students learn side-by-side with the faculty rather than in a traditional student-teacher classroom format. AB organizers recognized this and shifted the new program's design to conform to the ideal, inviting outside artists and craftspeople onto campus to teach students and teachers alike. Today this system continues, with all Holderness School participants pushing their creative comfort zones together under artists-in-residence. During the length of the AB program, the school also attends evening performances by visiting artists.

There was still a wrinkle to be ironed out, however. Though the school's goal was to provide a unique experience to every student during the March Special Programs, some students were participating in AB for a third time by their senior year. The solution was to add a new program: Senior Colloquium. This program, begun in 1981, exposed seniors to a rigorous academic experience comparable to one they might have in college.[463] Seniors now spent these weeks in March focusing on a particular topic under the guidance of the faculty. For many years, the Senior Colloquium coursework centered on a single theme ("Science and Human Values"[464] or "The Twenties,"[465] for example). Today, participating seniors choose from a selection of Colloquium course offerings, which may or may not have a common thread.

The last program, begun in 1990 by faculty member Mark Perkins, was service-oriented—in its first year, twenty-one sophomores and five faculty members worked with the Habitat for Humanity program.[466] It was a great success, and the program continued to expand in size. By 1999, some students were traveling to work at Habitat for Humanity sites, while others performed similar labor in the Interfaith Housing Corporation's work camps.[467] Today, participating sophomores choose from several service opportunities offered during the Special Programs period.

The four Special Programs that take place during the March period allow students to challenge themselves in a unique way every year at Holderness School. New students immerse themselves in AB, discovering unexplored creative fronts. Sophomores learn to expand their capacity for service and volunteerism. Juniors challenge themselves physically and spiritually during their OB trip. Seniors push themselves intellectually through Senior Colloquium coursework. The Special Programs thus cumulatively represent the skills that Holderness School hopes to encourage in its graduates: creativity, spirituality, athleticism, and intellectualism.

ATHLETICS AND THE OUTDOORS

Competitive Athletics

The earliest athletes at Holderness School competed with each other rather than with other schools. Long before students traveled to play outside teams, intramural sports existed as pick-up games vying with other recreational activities like hiking or card-playing. Interest in team sports only increased, however, and by the late 1880s, students were organizing school clubs, or "associations," around athletics.

Sometimes these associations were umbrella organizations, like the Holderness School Athletic Association (or HSAA). This group was not team-specific, but helped to organize events like the annual school field day competitions. All participating athletes were expected to pay dues to the HSAA, although the contributions could not always be relied upon. One school article complained:

> Certain members of the school have openly declared that unless they are put in such and such a division, a division suitable to themselves, they decline to pay any dues. In other words they object to enter anything on Field Day unless they are positively sure of a harvest of prizes.[468]

Other associations did not face this same difficulty, as they were created by interested parties to support the individual sports that those parties enjoyed. This meant that, as long as interest in a sport survived, its association was likely to receive adequate funds. However, an association for one sport might fade from view if interest was diverted to another recreation. The Holderness School Lawn Tennis Association, for example, felt a squeeze in the spring of 1888 because "at that time everything, and anything, was baseball."[469] However, enough student interest helped it survive to subsidize the creation of some on-campus courts and sponsor an intramural tournament or two.

Baseball and football both got their start with the formation of a few on-campus teams that most frequently played each other. Students were impatient for the opportunity to play outside teams before they could secure support from the school's administration to do so:

> Unless we propose to compete in harmless match games with the [baseball] nines of neighboring towns, we greatly fear a diminished interest, if not a total neglect showed for the game. We then sincerely indorse [sic] such a movement and trust all impediments will be removed for the manager so to act.[470]

The administration acceded, and Holderness School athletes were soon playing town teams from Plymouth and Ashland, or teams from nearby schools of the time such as the Haverhill Institute and Tilton Seminary.[471]

Baseball game in front of campus buildings, circa 1895

Squads which traveled to outside competitions were the first "official" teams from Holderness School. Sports organizations that held only on-campus matches (such as the first tennis associations) were destined to remain recreational activities for some time. Such activities would fade in and out of view over the years based on student interest.

From the inception of competitive sports at Holderness School, football and baseball dominated athletics. During the winters, students continued to play pick-up games of basketball and hockey or explore the recreational activities of the area ("sliding on sleds and skees" and snowshoeing) rather than participating in any organized teams.[472] This changed around 1902, however, when the official Holderness School basketball squad made its debut.[473] Its introduction meant that each season now offered a single athletic team to dominate student interest: football in the fall, basketball in the winter, and baseball in the spring. This was an effective model that stayed in place for some time.

In the 1920s, competitive athletics at Holderness School finally began to diversify. New teams in cross-country running[474], hockey[475], tennis[476], and track[477] meant that students could choose an alternative sports option during every season. In 1935, under Weld, both golf[478] and downhill skiing[479] became competitive sports rather than recreation. Of course, as student interests changed, sports teams adjusted. Skiing began to branch out into different specializations during Hagerman's time. Hagerman also approved the addition of teams in soccer[480], wrestling[481], sailing[482], rock climbing[483] and lacrosse.[484] With the advent of boarding coeducation in the late 1970s, Holderness School athletics needed to reflect the change. Woodward ensured that the school embraced not only new girls' teams in traditional athletics, but also sports that were novel to the school, such as field hockey[485] and softball.[486]

Not every team that was approved continued indefinitely. Some teams that exist today have had only intermittent histories at the school (basketball, golf and cycling all fall into this category). Other teams, such as sailing and wrestling, are no longer competitive sports at all. Although some teams lack permanent staying power, the notion of choice does not: since the 1920s, Holderness School students have been able to choose from multiple athletic options during each season.

Snow Sports

Holderness School is well-known for its outstanding snow sports program. Students are encouraged to take full advantage of the school's beautiful location in the White Mountains, and an impressive number go on to excel in national and international competition. Holderness School is not a ski academy, however. Rather, it attracts students who want to balance a valuable sports experience with the academic and social aspects of school life.

In the school's early days, students used their free time to explore the surrounding terrain and enjoy the natural beauty of the area. Long winters were endemic to the area, and students embraced snowball fights, tobogganing, snowshoeing, skating, and skiing. Although Holderness School sports teams were formed as early as the 1890s, winter pastimes were not organized competitively for many years. In 1916, the school outfitted its first hockey team, but skiing was still seen as a way to experience the outdoors rather than as a competitive sport.

Skier on Joy Hill, circa 1908

In 1929–30, however, this began to change. In that year the board welcomed new Trustee John Carleton, who had been a member of the 1928 American Olympic Winter Sports Team.[487] Perhaps as a result of Carleton's presence, and of the fresh perspective of headmaster Edric Weld, the profile of skiing at the school began to rise. By 1933, the school had added 200 acres to its fifteen-acre campus, and began developing its own ski trails.[488]

Competitive skiing was not far behind. Weld approved the formation of the first ski team in 1936, and the school never looked back.[489] Holderness students quickly built a ski jump and ski cabin, and François Bertrand (of the University of Grenoble) was hired as the school's first ski instructor.[490] In those early days of the ski program, instructor turnover was rapid. Between 1937 and 1943, Bertrand's successors included Anton Kolb, Edward Schaar, Karl Wernert, and Wendell Stephenson.[491] Stephenson (also a member of the school faculty) shepherded the team until 1951, when a turning point in the ski program was reached.[492]

In that year, Hagerman became the eighth headmaster at Holderness School, bringing Don Henderson with him.[493] Hagerman hoped that by investing even more in the ski program, the school could capitalize on its beautiful location and attract even higher numbers of applicants.[494] He believed that Henderson was the man for the job. A history teacher, Middlebury alum, and future Fulbright Exchange Teacher, Henderson understood the importance of balancing athletics with academics. He also was a world-class skier.

Because of this skill, Henderson occasionally balanced his time at Holderness with coaching roles at the highest levels. An Alpine coach at the 1964 Winter Olympics, Henderson was also head coach of the World Cup National Team from 1969–1970. From 1956 to 1984, every Winter Olympics included at least one athlete who had benefited from his coaching (a remarkable nine of these Olympic athletes were Holderness alumni).[495]

Holderness skiing—already considered by some to be "the most popular" sport on campus—benefited enormously from Henderson's leadership and experience. During his tenure, two downhill slopes were bushwhacked, a new tow rope and ski jump were built, and Holderness students began to participate in championship competitions at every level.[496] What had begun as an eight-member team in 1951 grew to almost twenty times that size by the time Henderson left the faculty in 1987.[497]

The program had also diversified and expanded to support new teams. Recreational skiers officially broke away from the competitive skiers in 1960, when Robert Linscott became the first Coordinator of Recreational Skiing.[498] The Alpine and Nordic teams split around 1966; the four-event format had shifted and competitions had become more specialized.[499] When ski jumping—an event long associated with the Nordic team—gained momentum around 1987, their results were tracked separately as well.[500]

This trend of expansion continued into the next decade. As a new generation of ski instructors became integral to Holderness, a new breed of snow sport was also emerging. Snowboarding was considered by some to be an "extreme" sport, but nevertheless was increasingly popular. In the 1989–90 school year, the first Holderness School snowboarders competed as a team.[501] Their success then and over the next decade helped to lay the foundation for the equally cutting-edge Freestyle team (begun in 1997–98)[502] and Free Skier X team (begun in 2003–04).[503]

Perhaps more than anything else, this tradition of exploration and growth is what typifies the snow sports program. Generations of students have used the program to experience the beauty of a northern winter first-hand. But more importantly, students have had the opportunity to push themselves and find new challenges on the slopes and trails near the school.

Outdoor Activities

In addition to the organized athletic teams at Holderness School, many non-competitive outdoor pastimes have been popular at the school. During the long winters before a structured snow sports program, much use was made of the abundant snow all the same—boys would skate, sled, and snowshoe, sometimes in large groups:

> [Headmaster Gray] had a large sled built, like an ice-boat, called the Pinafore, steered by a wheel, accommodating eighteen boys, and merry parties coasted down the winding hill from the front of the school to the intervale below. Two of the school horses dragged the heavy sled, for it would have been a weary work otherwise.[504]

In temperate weather, boys in these early years would swim or go May-flowering with friends.[505] Walking was also extremely popular, with students making jaunts across the intervale, up local mountains, and to Livermore Falls or Trinity Church.

Occasionally, students made longer treks, which, though requiring special permission, were well worth the extra effort. These sorts of trips could fill an entire weekend day, as one boy's journal entry attests:

> Moore and I got permission to go to Asquam Lake and [were] gone all day. We got a lunch of Mrs. Thompson and started. After we had gone about two miles we overtook Hubbard, Van Sands, and Guild and went on with them.

When we got there Merrill and Hutchins had got there first and hired the boat but we hired it of them and had it the rest of the day. They took Moore and I down the lake about two miles and back, and then we took the rest of the fellows once. Went into Big Asquam—there the wind was blowing quite hard and the waves were about four feet high, and Van Sands was "frightened to death." We ate our dinner at Huffs camp and there we found a sail boat, and Moore [took] a ride. Paid .40 for boat. Started back at four o'clock. Burned my forehead terribly.[506]

Winter weather was not necessarily a barrier to day-long outings. Here, a student describes a February 1883 hike to the top of Mount Prospect:

Mrs. Gray put us up a splendid dinner and we started at quarter of nine [...] We followed the road fast way up the mountain, and then took a short cut. When halfway up we had to take off our snow shoes and break holes through the crust with the feet. It was smooth, and if we had made a mis-step we would have slid down the mountain for half a mile. At last we reached the top and got a hold of the signal pole, and then started down the mountain. We followed our old tracks and thus we saved a great deal of time. The view from the top was beautiful. We could see about forty miles across the country [...] After eating our dinner we stayed about half an hour. We put on our snow shoes and then we came right along and arrived safely at the school at four o'clock. [507]

It is easy to consider hikes like these to be the forerunners of one of the oldest school traditions: Mountain Day. As early as 1907, students were taking advantage of special headmasters' holidays to climb mountains[508], and by 1927 the entire school was organizing for such trips.[509] The tradition became an annual—sometimes biannual—outing known as Mountain Day in the following decades, and the practice endures to the present day.

Camp Life

Another Holderness School tradition grew out of a multi-season activity: camp building. The daughter of first headmaster Gray remembered her father promoting this particular pastime:

[M]y father through the consent of neighboring farmers, encouraged the boys to build little camps in nearby woods rather than have them go to Plymouth a mile away [...]. On Saturday [afternoons] they had lunch there frequently,

cooked flap-jacks, often inviting my father. In this way he could see that there
was no over-stepping the courtesy extended. He thoroughly enjoyed it.[510]

Early camps began as underground dugouts where students "met and cooked
their oysters, drank coffee and attempted to make and eat any dainty dish they
could think of."[511] Building styles progressed over time, with dugouts replaced
first by at least one impressively solid log camp, and then by forts built of "boards
and planks," which remained the construction materials of choice.[512] Though
this more complex form of camp building was primarily a recreational activity, it
was also seen as bringing side benefits to students:

> The nature-loving spirit of the boys became general. All who had enterprise
> desired to possess a forest home: and even those who had little enterprise were
> challenged to join in the general craze and to work out of doors. Many a sickly
> fellow found his daily chopping and open-air labors better than a dozen doc-
> tor's prescriptions; and even an odd stomach ache on account of an overdose
> of flapjacks never diminished his daily strengthening.[513]

Over the years the forest camps evolved into something akin to secret societies,
with initiations and names that were publicly represented only by acronyms.
These fellowships were renewed every fall, and camp life continued right through
the winter months and into warm weather again. On even the bitterest winter
days students made expeditions through the snow-covered woods to read books
or enjoy feasts and good company around their communal campfires.[514]

The camp tradition extended beyond the academic year. In 1881 Ernest Balch
(an elder son of Holderness School patron Emily Balch) began what has been
called the very first resident boys' summer camp in America, located on Chocorua Island in Squam Lake.[515] Ernest had siblings who were educated under
headmaster Gray, and it is likely that some boys from Holderness School
attended his camp. Certainly they were familiar with it, as at least one student
account from the period describes rowing across the lake to the camp during an
outing with classmates.[516]

We know for certain that there were strong ties between Holderness School
and other summer camps. In 1889, Holderness School faculty members C.K.
Mellen and William S. Hubbard began Camp Sunapee (Hubbard was an alumnus who had been among the first to implement the board-building technique on
school camps).[517] Headmaster Webster himself began Camp Wachusett on
Squam Lake in 1903[518], and another faculty member began a camp on Stinson
Lake around 1904.[519] Holderness students often attended these summer camps,

which only increased an appreciation for the outdoors that had been instilled during the school year.

The notion of camp life as a formal extra-curricular organization slowly faded over the years. However, interest in camp building did not. Even when the activity was no longer condoned by the school administration, rumors of secret forts in the woods circulated at regular intervals. As late as the 1980s, evidence of unsanctioned camps was occasionally being discovered. Clearly the attraction of a private retreat in the New Hampshire woods does not weaken with the passage of time. Happily, the school provides students with other outlets for exploring and enjoying the magnificence of the local area.

Stewardship

Organizations such as the Rock Climbing, Mountaineering, and Outing Clubs of the 1970s were outgrowths of the school's affection for the natural beauty of its surroundings. During this time, the school community also showed its care for the outdoors by acknowledging the responsibility inherent to participating in such activities. Out Back participants were taught how to hike and camp without impacting the environment; students participated in initiatives to minimize campus energy use; awareness of the need for environmental conservation increased dramatically.

Three Ponds fishing trip that led to an all-school Mountain Day cleanup, 1973

The Outing Club provides a good example of how this heightened awareness affected student actions. Outing Club members, whose primary focus was trekking up nearby peaks, began to take notice of the effects human activities were having upon wilderness areas. When the club made a fishing trip in 1973, for example, students noted in the log that "there was a lot more than snow left—trash, trash, trash. It was quite a sight and a few of us decided that it would take at least a hundred people to clean up the ponds in a day's work. And the idea grew!" Eleven days later, the school traveled back to this area for an Outing Club-sponsored Mountain Day, and the faculty and students removed about two tons of trash.[520]

The new sense of responsibility generated during this era permeated the school deeply and left a lasting mark. The school's faculty and administration sought to incorporate environmental awareness into the curriculum, and with funding from the Dodge Foundation, launched a Center for Environmental Education (CEE) as part of the school's centennial celebrations. Kicking off the CEE's contributions was a Centennial Colloquium, which had environmental issues as its theme.[521] This symposium built on the school's long tradition of hosting guest speakers, and included talks on solar architecture, wastewater recycling, and predictions regarding society's environmental future.[522]

In addition to speaking forums, the CEE initiative was an umbrella for ecology and earth science classes, as well as for the construction of the bioshelter building. Designed by faculty members Bart and Sue Nourse, the bioshelter was "an energy-efficient, ecologically-derived, and low-cost solar home."[523] Its construction was completed by students under faculty guidance and was a massive undertaking, as this description of the first stages attests:

> Last fall the crew cleared and completed the excavation of the site, located on a south-facing slope off of Prospect Mountain Road. Next came the arduous tasks of (1) hand-digging a water-line trench to an existing well 280 feet uphill from the site, (2) collecting over twenty tons of local field stone to be used for the bearing/thermal mass walls, and (3) felling 11,000 board feet of pine and oak for framing, siding, and decking. Hauled out by horses, the timbers were milled locally at a tremendous savings. Next, while some students built thirty "slipforms" for the stone and concrete work, others dug the root cellar pit. The basement walls then rose to ground level, were covered by a deck fitted with a trap door, and—as the snows began—members of the post-and-beam frame were fashioned.[524]

The hands-on experience was meant to expose participating students to environmentally friendly systems and practices.[525]

Without faculty prompting, many students have also chosen to incorporate environmental issues into their senior projects. Seniors have become involved with New Hampshire's Forest Fish and Game Services (1979)[526], worked to reclaim the school's Frog Pond (1986)[527], studied outdoor education programs (1990)[528], and helped battle milfoil in Squam Lake (2004).[529] Even when no academic reward can result, students have embraced environmental stewardship. Volunteers on school energy committees[530] or members of extra-curricular organizations such as the Recycle-Bulls, for example, give their own time in order to keep conservation activities and issues in the thoughts of fellow students.[531]

The physical setting of Holderness School has helped define the school's character perhaps more than any other factor. The school certainly tries to instill an appreciation for the outdoors through recreation. However, students also take away powerful life lessons about their own potential for growth and stewardship. The impact of the environment on students' intellectual, spiritual, and physical experiences cannot be denied. From snow sports team members to students who are committed to preserving the environment, few graduates have left untouched by the beauty of the school's surroundings.

ARTS AND EXTRA-CURRICULARS

Reaching Out

As with the development of athletics, artistic and extra-curricular organizations at Holderness School were an outgrowth of activities pursued by students for personal entertainment. In some cases, informal gatherings in dorm rooms eventually developed into clubs or performing groups. The driving factor behind even the more organized activities remained the enjoyment of the participants.

In an 1883 journal, a Holderness School student mentions games like euchre and marbles are mentioned as pleasant ways to spend an evening with friends. Impromptu concerts or dress-up parties were also options to pass the time. The latter occupations can be seen as the seeds of more formalized school activities. The boy describes practicing on his harmonica and getting pointers from a peer: "Small learned me two or three times on my instrument."[532] Collaborations similar to these, perhaps, led to the formation of early student musical groups such as the Ocarina Quartette of 1889[533] or the Banjo Club of 1890.[534]

There are several indications that there was a strong interest in theatrical performance from the very start of the school. Clyde Fitch, who attended Holderness School during its first year, went on to become an acclaimed playwright: he
produced over fifty plays, over half of which were original.[535] While a student,
Fitch was responsible for staging productions of The Lady of Lyons and Patience,
"the cast of the latter including nearly half the school."[536]

Not long afterward, another Holderness School student was preparing for a
career in theater. Maclyn Arbuckle, cousin of performer Fatty Arbuckle and a
future theater and movie actor, attended an 1883 dorm gathering where "some of
the boys dressed up;" a friend noted that "Arbuckle was the best" of the boys in
costume.[537] Spontaneous costume contests such as this, as well as grass-roots play
productions like those Fitch had staged, were essentially forerunners of structured
theatrical organizations at the school. By the 1890s, a Holderness School Dramatic Association had been established.[538]

Other casual social gatherings also grew into extra-curricular organizations
during this time. For example, the outdoor camps that headmaster Gray encouraged his students to build evolved into clubs with official members and mot-
tos.[539] Boys also had the option of joining fraternities or secret societies, which
published alumni rolls and engravings of their shields in the school annual.[540]
Students with similar hobbies created clubs around their interests: the Photography, Chess, and Chemical Clubs were just a few of these.[541]

These new organizations indicated that tradition and school culture was developing at the young institution. Celebrations during the Easter holiday began to
incorporate variety show and theatrical performances by students.[542] The school
choir and other musical organizations became a regular feature of Closing Day
festivities.[543] New school publications like the Volunteer and the Argus recorded
notable events, athletic results, and student literary efforts.

These activities were also notable because, although primarily targeted to the
on-campus audience, they were open to the broader school community. Parents,
friends, and residents of nearby towns were likely to attend performances during
holiday or commencement celebrations. Alumni would frequently subscribe to
school magazines to keep current with school life. In fact, during the school's
twenty-fifth anniversary, a special school annual called the Red and White was
distributed to returning alumni.[544] Student activities—particularly those related
to the arts—provided a way to connect with people outside of campus and com-
municate school culture.

Providing Direction

During its first fifty years, Holderness School did not incorporate fine arts into the official curriculum. Students engaged in music, theater, and the visual arts primarily through extra-curricular organizations (all three fields could be explored during the design and performance of school musicals, for example). As the 1930s approached, however, the school began to emphasize the importance of the arts. During Weld's first year as headmaster, fine arts courses titled <u>Arts and Crafts of the Ages</u> and <u>The Appreciation of Painting</u> were added to the curriculum.[545] The school catalog asserted that extra-curricular activities were not only outlets for entertainment, but also opportunities for self-improvement:

Students creating pottery (left) and metalwork (right), circa 1934

Holderness would give the boy an education for leisure time (one of our greatest deficiencies today) by furnishing the opportunities for the appreciation of great literature, music, and art, which will be a constant source of enjoyment through his entire life. [...] Holderness life [also] includes opportunities for self-expression in hand crafts of all sorts, drawing and painting, playing in an

orchestra or individually, singing in glee club or choir, dramatics, and the
school magazine. Every boy is encouraged to develop a hobby.[546]

With the school acknowledging the value of exposing students to the arts, faculty members were soon acting as mentors for related activities. In some cases,
faculty members did so through their formal teaching role. By 1934, for example,
Holderness School offered classes in manual training and mechanical drawing, in
addition to the art history and appreciation courses mentioned above.[547] Faculty
members also acted as more informal advisors to extra-curricular activities, as
when teachers Avery Rogers, Charles Abbey, and William Judge helped to coordinate annual student productions of Gilbert & Sullivan operettas.[548] Whether as
teachers or advisors, the school's faculty members were helping to shape students'
experiences of what had previously been purely recreational activities.

It is important to note that there have always been clubs *not* related to the arts
that also relied heavily on a faculty advisor. The debate club of the 1940s, which
flourished under Charles Abbey, is a good example. The current incarnation of
the school yearbook is another. However, most of the early faculty-sponsored
clubs (such as the Glee Club and Gilbert & Sullivan organizations) were linked
to the fine arts.

The school also sought to encourage students' artistic interests by hosting lec-
turers and performers. While the school also invited guests to speak on academi-
cally-oriented topics, a significant portion of the presentations were related to the
arts. These widely varied talks involved visits from makeup artists[549],
cartoonists[550], musicians[551], magicians[552], scholars[553], and others. Additionally,
the school encouraged students to experience off-campus performances, such as
those given in the concert series at Dartmouth College.[554]

Both the incorporation of the arts into the formal curriculum and the
increased support of faculty for arts-related activities were significant developments. The changes drew a new distinction between those extra-curricular activities driven purely by student interest and those encouraged (in some cases,
guided) by the faculty. The result was the increased prominence of artistic activities throughout school life.

School production of Gilbert & Sullivan's "H.M.S. Pinafore," 1940

Today, the school continues to stress the importance of the arts to student development. All freshmen and new sophomores participate in Artward Bound during the Special Programs period, and traditional coursework is offered in photography, music, ceramics, drawing, theater, and more. Certain of these courses are geared specifically toward performances or gallery installations, to be presented outside of class time. This reflects the close connection that Holderness School's curricular and extra-curricular arts activities have had for some time.

Building Support

Around the time that arts courses were introduced into the Holderness School curriculum, new goals for students were being articulated. The catalogue stressed classroom education, religious life, and athletic recreation, but also pointed out that students "must be led out by being given opportunities for self-expression" in creative pastimes.[555] With creativity openly acknowledged as an important facet of education, the arts took on a new significance at Holderness School.

The school first provided for students' creative development by increasing support for extra-curricular activities and by adding some academic courses, as described above. The arts and the art curriculum grew deeper roots over time. By the 1946–1947 academic year, seven of the nineteen faculty members were involved in teaching arts courses. Of the seven, three devoted their teaching solely to the fine arts curriculum.[556]

One of these faculty members was Herbert Waters, who joined the school as an established artist in his own right. Waters had already been widely recognized for his outstanding woodcuts and watercolors, and he continued to win acclaim for his work throughout his time at Holderness School.[557] Waters was joined by Ellie Stark, Bertha Waters (his wife), and other talented artists during this period. In essence, the school had created its first arts department around a less traditional approach to teaching art, where students learned under master teachers:

> Our work room is run as a studio rather than as a classroom. We aim at an atmosphere of art work in continuous production, work carried on by instructors as well as students. The instructors may be working on their own professional work, or on a student problem about a week in advance of the boys (possibly introducing a new media). Things to draw or paint or model, the materials to work with, are always ready and waiting.[558]

Waters remained a part of the school faculty until 1961, and rejoined the school on a limited basis again during the 1970s.[559] During this span of time, visual arts opportunities at Holderness School had grown to include photography, ceramics, printmaking, painting, woodworking, and sculpture.[560] Theater and music were also slowly gaining momentum, acquiring part-time instructors as well as faculty advisors for related clubs.

When headmaster Woodward came to Holderness School, he appreciated the unique value that practicing artists like Waters had provided to the school's arts program. In expanding the department, he made a conscious decision to pursue more such teachers.[561] The result was a new generation of talented and prolific artists in the department, which now formally encompassed music and drama in addition to the visual arts. The Artward Bound program, begun in 1979, further embraced the concept of apprenticeship to master artists, and AB quickly became a staple experience for students and faculty alike.

Although the growth of the arts at Holderness School has been steady, the commitment to hiring practicing artists as faculty presents its own challenges. As Waters explained to headmaster Hagerman, such faculty members are "essentially Lonely [sic]:"

The over-all life of a boy's school runs—in casual conversation [of] both faculty and boys—towards athletics—and the art man, or poet—etc. feels he and his work are not valued, and often are down-rated, even laughed at. And yet, in his bones, he Knows [sic], some boys there will be changed for life, and some Faculty nourished in the needs they have, too. [562]

The difficulty in acclimating to the essentially foreign environment of a boarding school can be compounded by the school's demands on faculty time. For practicing artists, such demands can make it extremely difficult to pursue the professional work for which they were hired. The school has done its best to compensate for this challenge by enabling arts faculty members to take time for sabbaticals or professional development whenever possible.

Such opportunities have been essential for teachers like Waters, who believed strongly that, over time, teaching without time for professional work sapped his creative "sources of strength." He expressed gratitude that his "long-cherished hope of [...] freedom for creative work without interruptions" was facilitated by the school.[563] Current arts faculty members like David Lockwood and Franz Nicolay have been in an even better position to pursue such opportunities, as more support is available through sources such as the Van Otterloo Faculty Development Fund.[564]

Of course, the arts faculty also need to be supported by school facilities. In the early years of the arts program at Holderness School, studios were located in basement spaces of buildings such as Livermore Hall and Rathbun Dormitory.[565] In 1974, the fine arts department finally gained a dedicated building when the venerable Carpenter Gymnasium was converted from an athletic facility and made available.[566] Though this initial renovation marked a step in the right direction for arts facilities, the space was still not ideal. Faculty member David Lockwood recalled his teaching experiences in Carpenter during his early days at Holderness School:

[Carpenter] had a makeshift, make-do quality when I arrived in the early eighties. My classrooms had no heat other than what rose from the art room below and if I forgot to open the plywood flaps in the chorus room the night before, the singers could see their breath in the morning. Rehearsals were deafening and in an effort to reduce the din in our cramped, cold triangular room, I scrounged up two hundred and fifty egg cartons from the kitchen and stapled them to the walls as rudimentary soundproofing. The art room was below us and during rehearsals, whenever the drums, electric guitars, keyboards and horns stopped playing, we would hear Emily Zabransky still shouting at the top of her lungs in a gallant effort to be heard over our racket, kind of like Wile E. Coyote out past the edge of the cliff, legs whirring.[567]

A concerted effort to improve facilities for the arts department was underway, however. The process began when an auditorium was integrated with the design of 1984's Hagerman Science Building; the stage has been used by theater students ever since.[568] A decade later, a much more extensive renovation of the old gym produced the Carpenter Center for the Arts and the Edward Arts Gallery. The clever repurposing of existing space, and the addition of an area devoted to art installations, marked a new era at Holderness School. For the first time, art and music students had access to "a wonderful home for creativity," one that was "dynamic and inspiring, complete with big open spaces and intimate nooks."[569] The later gift of a recording studio has also made it possible for students to work on special musical projects. Even using only half of the recording projects that go through the studio each year, the school is able to release a compact disc showcasing student work about every other year.[570]

The story of the arts at Holderness School is one of consistent growth and improvement, but also one of balance. The school strives to support its artistic, academic, athletic, and spiritual programs equally; faculty members struggle to balance lives as practicing artists with their responsibilities as members of the school community. The inherent challenges of these tensions could, in some environments, inhibit success. However, the result at Holderness School has been a dynamic, energized atmosphere of creativity, in which students are exposed to both new media and deeply committed artists on a daily basis.

A Vision for the Future

In 2001, the school entered the new millennium in a position of strength. New Head of School R. Phillip Peck has more resources at hand than any previous headmaster: no debt, a healthy endowment, an impressive physical plant, engaged trustees, supportive parents, motivated faculty, and talented students. In fact, the school has never been so strong.

Head of School Phil Peck, 2004

And yet, like his predecessors, Peck is committed to looking beyond the school's current successes in order to assure a better future. During his induction speech, he called on the school community to do three things: live a life of reflection, pay attention to detail, and care for others. By keeping these three guidelines relevant to day-to-day activities, the school can be successful in all of its missions. In particular, Peck's call for members of the school to care for each other is central to daily campus life. In the Holderness School community, people know the names of everyone they pass on the paths, student leaders take assembly time to recognize hard working job crews, and visitors comment regularly on the friendly helpfulness of students.

The attitude of caring necessarily reaches beyond the bounds of campus. Students volunteer at local churches and community organizations, and do their part to forge strong relationships with surrounding towns.[571] And as in the past, these communities continue to provide a model of the kind of loving support to which the school aspires. In January of 2003, the school tragically lost two students in a hit and run by a drunk driver. Even as students, faculty, and the boys' families comforted each other, support poured in from people throughout the state and beyond. Letters of encouragement and condolence came from families, friends, fellow schools, and even from ostensible strangers to Holderness School. Within twelve days, a new scholarship fund had received more than $25,000 from over a thousand donors. In one remarkable show of support, the students of Plymouth Regional High School donated $1,000 raised entirely through the sale of $1 memorial lapel ribbons.[572]

Such times of crisis challenge a school, testing the depth and worth of its traditions. By insisting on a culture that centers on caring, the administration strengthens the school's resilience and ability to survive even the most painful experiences. Although this is of primary importance, sometimes more mundane challenges can threaten a school's well-being as well. For this reason, it is important to look ahead and plan strategically for the future. Peck has embraced this process as well, applying the three guidelines outlined in his induction speech to his own role at the school.

Believing that a school must reflect on its own achievements in order to identify its strengths and weaknesses, Peck solicited voices from across the school community and used the resulting perspectives to shape a new strategic plan for the school. The goals laid out in that plan provide a general roadmap for progress at the school, and the next step involves pinpointing ways to achieve those goals. In other words, the school must now pay attention to the details. While some strategies have already been identified, there will be fine points to work out for many years to come.

Much of the work to come will circle around the key objectives identified in the strategic plan. The first of these goals is to continue to build a "vibrant intellectual culture."[573] Without conscious attention, the academic and creative aspects of school culture can decline. To underscore the importance of the life of the mind, the school is focusing on strengthening academic departments and curricula, providing increased support for the arts, and integrating technology with the curriculum and with professional development opportunities.[574]

Achievements have already begun in these areas. All teaching faculty members have received laptops for school use, accompanied by training in computer literacy and in the integration of technology with department-specific curricula.[575] The school has formed a new joint committee of faculty and board members, whose mandate is to identify ways in which the academic life of the school can be enhanced. As part of this initiative, Peck would like to ensure that every senior at the school undergoes a transformative intellectual experience. To achieve this, the school may restructure the Senior Colloquium and Senior Project options, or it may create an entirely new opportunity to challenge seniors. In either case, Peck anticipates building stronger ties between academic year curricula and the events experienced by each class during the Special Programs period in March.

The strategic plan also acknowledges that the school must continue to retain "a versatile and accomplished faculty and staff" if it is to maintain quality.[576] The trustees and administration are committed to identifying individuals who can serve in a variety of roles, and to supporting their efforts to the fullest extent possible. The strategic plan calls for the school to continue providing competitive compensation in the areas of "salary, benefits, professional development, work load, and other living and working conditions" in order to do so.[577]

During faculty recruitment, the school remains committed to addressing issues of gender parity and ethnic diversity. At the start of Pete Woodward's tenure, the school had only two women on its teaching faculty.[578] When he left the school, the number was at fourteen and rising.[579] Peck is dedicated to continuing this growth, and is supported by the school's trustees. These values are reflected in the current composition of the board, which currently includes eight female board members.[580] One of these women is Piper Orton '74, who was elected the first woman chair of the board in 2004.[581]

The school is also committed to identifying qualified candidates of color for the faculty, staff and student populations. The strategic plan recognizes that, for a school to thrive, it must have community members of diverse gender, ethnicity, geography, national origin, sexual orientation, talent, and socio-economic backgrounds:[582]

> A diverse Holderness community [...] provides a richer and more wide-ranging educational environment; it ensures that the School remains responsive to its changing regional, national and international environments; it enables people to learn to participate in a community that encompasses several dimensions of diversity; and it prepares students for the world beyond Holderness.[583]

The addition of a Deans-level Director of Diversity position, the creation of web pages devoted to issues of diversity, and the development of the FOCUS Student Diversity Council all are recent steps taken on the path toward achieving these ends.[584]

The physical plant of Holderness School has been radically improved over the last twenty years. Nevertheless, the school must continue to address issues of "size, health, safety, and information access" in order to maintain this success.[585] To this end, two major undertakings have already been accomplished during Peck's tenure.

First, the renovation of Livermore Hall was completed in January of 2004. This remarkable project included the construction of a new Health Center on the building's lowest level, where overnight care and on-campus counseling facilities constitute just a portion of the health services available to students.[586] Second, a multi-year initiative to improve the technology infrastructure on campus has resulted in wireless internet connectivity for all of the dormitory and academic buildings on campus.[587] New filtering policies and equipment provide control over both the times that student internet access is available, and the content that can be accessed from the dorm.[588] This allows the school to implement the technology thoughtfully and in coordination with the school's overall mission.

The school will continue to address the needs of the physical plant as it moves forward. One goal is to improve pedestrian safety, and a multi-phased plan to achieve this is already underway. Tunnels have been installed to connect the main campus both with the Gallop/Bartsch athletic facilities and with the lower fields; these have reduced the number of students crossing increasingly traffic-heavy Route 175. Further phases of the plan include expanded student parking, improvements to the chapel lane access route to Plymouth and the lower tunnel, and the completion of fencing along Route 175.[589]

A last, crucial goal stated in the strategic plan is to increase the school's revenue and endowment.[590] This accomplishment is vital to the well-being of the school. As we have seen in the past, economic volatility can threaten a school's very existence; only a healthy endowment for people, programs, and facilities can guarantee that an institution will weather unexpected financial storms. More importantly, an increased endowment decreases the dependence that a school has on tuition income. It results in "a more talented and diverse pool of admissions candidates" by imparting the freedom to accept students based solely on talent, rather than on their financial needs.[591]

The goals embraced by Peck, the trustees, and the administration provide an outline for the next chapter in the school's history. Issues of academic strength, quality faculty, diversity, and economic stability must maintain their attention if the school is to move forward. Certainly no school can afford to rest on its laurels without risking stagnation and irrelevancy, and for this reason the school remains focused on progress.

Insisting that the school has the capacity for improvement, however, does not minimize the accomplishments already achieved. On the contrary, the Holderness School community is well aware that the school is thriving in the present day. The school's culture of caring, and the academic, athletic, and creative achievements of its students, are a testament to that. However, it is the future that will determine the school's ultimate success. Self-examination and reflection, the identification of concrete methods for achieving goals, and the continued appreciation of the people in the community—these practices will help see the school through difficult times.

With careful planning, luck, and loving stewardship, Holderness School will flourish for at least another 125 years. A humble focus on self-improvement, as the school's opening sermon pointed out, is the best way to assure that success. As the school's story carries on, may "this tender vine" experience only the fruitful continuance aspired to on that day in 1879.

Notes

1. Frederick M. Gray, minutes of the meeting of the Holderness School Board of Trustees, ms., 4 Apr. 1882, Holderness School Archives, New Hampshire.

   Frederick M. Gray, minutes of the meeting of the Holderness School Board of Trustees, ms., 20 Sep. 1882, Holderness School Archives, New Hampshire.

2. Edric A. Weld, <u>Three-Quarter Mark: Holderness School 1879-1954</u> ([New Hampshire]: [Holderness School], 1954) 28.

3. Mayland H. Morse, Jr., "A Quarter-Century of Dedicated Service," 1 Sep. 1975, Holderness School Archives, New Hampshire.

4. Howard F. Hill, <u>A Sermon: Preached at the Opening of Holderness School for Boys</u> (Concord: The Republican Press Association, 1880) 10.

5. H. Hill 14.

6. Margaret A. Howe and Susan Bacon Keith, <u>An Abbreviated History of Holderness, New Hampshire, 1761–1961</u> ([New Hampshire]: [By Author], 1962) 4.

7. Howe and Keith 1.

8. Howe and Keith 4-5.

9. "Framers of Freedom: Samuel Livermore," <u>SeacoastNH.com</u>, 10 Oct. 2004 <http://www.seacoastnh.com/framers/livermore.html>.

10. Howe and Keith 4-6.

11. Mrs. Harrison F. Sargent, notes on Holderness history, ts., Holderness School Archives, New Hampshire, [1979?], [8].

12. Sargent [6, 8].

13. Sargent [8].

14. Sargent [8, 10].

15. Weld, Three-Quarter Mark 7.

16. "Sketch of Holderness," Ollapodrida '91 2 (1891): 74-75.

17. "History of Holderness–The Whiton Family," Holderness Historical Society Newsletter 6.1 (2000): [1].

18. "History of Holderness–The Whiton Family" [1-2].

19. "History of Holderness–The Whiton Family" [2].

20. "History of Holderness–The Whiton Family" [2].

21. "Sketch of Holderness" 74-75.

22. "Alumni Notes," The Dial 10.2 (Mar. 1932): 20

23. Sargent [2].

24. "William Woodruff Niles," Virtual American Biographies, 10 Oct. 2004 <http://www.famousamericans.net/williamwoodruffniles/>.

25. William Porter Niles, Fifty Years of Holderness School ([New Hampshire]: [Holderness School], n.d.) 1.

26. Niles 1.

27. Niles 1-2.

28. Albert C. Jacobs, "Holderness–Seventy-Five Years of a Splendid Tradition," address, Seventy-Fifth Anniversary of Holderness School, Holderness School, New Hampshire, 1 May 1954.

29. Niles 2-3.

30. Ezra S. Stearns, History of Plymouth New Hampshire, vol. 1 (Cambridge: The University Press, 1906) 190, 319-320.

31. Niles 3.

32. H.W. Blair, promissory note, ms., Holderness School Archives, New Hampshire, 23 Oct. 1880.

    Stearns 376-377.

33. H.W. Blair, supplementary proposal, ms., Holderness School Archives, New Hampshire, 31 Jul. 1878.

34. Niles 3.

35. Sargent [5].

36. [Eleanor M. Gray Stetson], notes on the history of Holderness School, ms., Holderness School Archives, New Hampshire, [c.1939].

37. F.A.G. Cowper, "Holderness School," The Argus 2.3 (May 1902): 26.

38. "Alumni Notes" 20.

39. "1888," Holderness Newsletter 2.2 (Dec. 1953): 2.

40. Cowper 26.

41. [Stetson].

42. Cowper 26.

43. Montrose J. Moses and Virginia Gerson, Clyde Fitch and His Letters (Boston: Little, Brown and Company, 1924) 9.

44. Moses and Gerson 15.

45. Holderness School for Boys, Plymouth, New Hampshire: Second Year (n.p.: n.p., [1880]) 3.

46. [Stetson].

47. George Baxter Underwood, "The Journal of George Baxter Underwood," unpublished transcript, 1883, Holderness School Archives, New Hampshire, 67.

48. Underwood 58.

49. Holderness School for Boys, Plymouth, New Hampshire: Fifth Year, 1883 (n.p.: n.p., 1883) 1.

50. George Olcott, minutes of the meeting of the Holderness School Board of Trustees, ms., 16 May 1879, Holderness School Archives, New Hampshire.

51. Frederick M. Gray, minutes of the meeting of the Holderness School Board of Trustees, ms., 15 May 1884, Holderness School Archives, New Hampshire.

52. [Stetson].

53. Cowper 26.

54. Cowper 26.

55. [Stetson].

56. Cowper 26.

57. Gray 20 Sep. 1882.

58. Holderness School Second Year 10.

59. Moses and Gerson 16.

60. Cowper 26.

61. Cowper 26-27.

62. Underwood 48.

63. Cowper 27.

64. Cowper 27.

65. Cowper 27.

66. Underwood 49.

67. William Stimpson Hubbard, "In Memory of Wm. Clyde Fitch '82," The Argus 9.2 (Dec. 1909) 14.

68. Underwood 86, 62, 55, 9, 53, 33.

69. Frank C. Coolbaugh, minutes of the meeting of the Holderness School Board of Trustees, ms., 24 Sep. 1890, Holderness School Archives, New Hampshire.

70. Weld, Three-Quarter Mark 9.

71. "Death of Rev. Dr. Coolbaugh," The Living Church n.p. ([c. 1921]).

72. Weld, Three-Quarter Mark 10.

73. Niles 6.

74. "Camps," Ollapodrida '92 3 (1892): 37-44.

    "Athletics," Ollapodrida '92 3 (1892): 45-52.

75. Weld, Three-Quarter Mark 9.

76. Editorial, The Volunteer 2.1 (Oct. 1888): 2.

77. Holderness School 1883 2.

78. Catalogue of Holderness School for Boys, Plymouth, N.H.: Twelfth Year, 1890-'91 (Concord, New Hampshire: Republican Press Association, 1891) 6.

79. Catalogue of the Holderness School, Plymouth, N.H.: Ninth Year, 1887 (Bethlehem, New Hampshire: Charles T. Ranlett, [1887]) 6.

80. Weld, Three-Quarter Mark 10.

81. Editorial, The Volunteer 2.2 (Nov. 1888): 1-2.

82. Editorial, The Volunteer 1.7 (June 1888): 3.

83. "Secret Societies," Ollapodrida '92 3 (1892): 23-35.

    "Camps," Ollapodrida '92 3 (1892): 37-44.

    "Athletics," Ollapodrida '92 3 (1892): 45-52.

    "Miscellaneous Organizations," Ollapodrida '92 3 (1892): 53-63.

84. "1888," Holderness Newsletter 4.2 (27 May 1954): 4.

85. Charles Aubrey Slosson, letter to Edric A. Weld, 25 Feb. 1954.

86. Charles A. Ranlett, letter to Edric A. Weld, 22 Feb. 1954.

87. Editorial, Volunteer 2.1 2.

88. "School Notes," The Volunteer 2.6 (Apr. 1889): 6.

89. Catalogue of the Holderness School, Plymouth, N.H.; Tenth Year, 1888 (Bethlehem, New Hampshire: Charles T. Ranlett, [1888]) 12-15.

90. Slosson 25 Feb. 1954.

91. "1890 and 1892," Holderness Newsletter 4.2 (27 May 1954): 3-4.

92. Editorial, The Volunteer 1.7 (June 1888): 3.

93. Catalogue of the Holderness School for Boys, Plymouth, N.H.: Thirteenth Year, 1891–'92 (Concord, New Hampshire: Republican Press Association, 1892) 11-12.

94. Frank C. Coolbaugh, minutes of the meeting of the Holderness School Board of Trustees, ms., 17 June 1891, Holderness School Archives, New Hampshire.

95. Cowper 27.

96. "School Notes," The Argus 6.4 (Feb. 1907): 55.

97. Frank C. Coolbaugh, letter to William Stimpson Hubbard, 14 Sep. 1920, Holderness School Archives, New Hampshire.

98. Coolbaugh 14 Sep. 1920.

99. "Holderness Head and Faculty," The Argus 16.5 (Jun. 1917): 4.

100. "1920," Holderness Newsletter 2.6 (Dec. 1957): 5.

101. Niles 6.

102. Lorin Webster, minutes of the meeting of the Holderness School Board of Trustees, ms., 8 Sep. 1892, Holderness School Archives, New Hampshire.

103. Lorin Webster, minutes of the meeting of the Holderness School Board of Trustees, ms., 2 Dec. 1892, Holderness School Archives, New Hampshire.

Lorin Webster, minutes of the meeting of the Holderness School Board of Trustees, ms., 24 May 1893, Holderness School Archives, New Hampshire.

Lorin Webster, minutes of the meeting of the Holderness School Board of Trustees, ms., 14 June 1894, Holderness School Archives, New Hampshire.

Lorin Webster, minutes of the meeting of the Holderness School Board of Trustees, ms., 5 June 1895, Holderness School Archives, New Hampshire.

104. Lorin Webster, minutes of the meeting of the Holderness School Board of Trustees, ms., 24 Sep. 1896, Holderness School Archives, New Hampshire.

105. Lorin Webster, minutes of the meeting of the Holderness School Board of Trustees, ms., 28 Sep. 1904, Holderness School Archives, New Hampshire.

Lorin Webster, minutes of the meeting of the Holderness School Board of Trustees, ms., 27 Sep. 1905, Holderness School Archives, New Hampshire.

106. Niles 6.

107. "Personals," The Argus 3.3 (Apr. 1903): 101.

108. "Holderness School Song," The Argus 4.1 (Feb. 1904): 228-229.

109. "Editorials," The Argus 13.6-7 (Apr.-May 1914): 102.

110. Lorin Webster, minutes of the meeting of the Holderness School Board of Trustees, ms., 8 Feb. 1901, Holderness School Archives, New Hampshire.

Lorin Webster, minutes of the meeting of the Holderness School Board of Trustees, ms., 8 Nov. 1901, Holderness School Archives, New Hampshire.

111. Catalogue of Holderness School for Boys, Plymouth, N.H.: Twenty-Fourth Year, 1902–03 (Concord, New Hampshire: The Rumford Press, 1903) 5.

112. Weld, Three-Quarter Mark 14.

113. Weld, Three-Quarter Mark 13.

114. Weld, Three-Quarter Mark 13.

115. "1918," Holderness Newsletter 2.1 (Dec. 1952): 3.

116. "Holderness During the Past Year," The Argus 5.5 (Jun. 1905): 63.

117. Weld, Three-Quarter Mark 16.

118. Lorin Webster, minutes of the meeting of the Holderness School Board of Trustees, ms., 26 May 1908, Holderness School Archives, New Hampshire.

119. "School Notes," The Argus 5.12 (May 1906): 200.

120. "Editorials," The Argus 8.6-7 (Apr.-May 1914): 102.

121. Catalogue of Holderness School for Boys, Plymouth, New Hampshire: Thirty-Fourth Year, 1912–13 (Peterborough, New Hampshire: Transcript Printing Co., 1913) 6.

122. Lorin Webster, minutes of the meeting of the Holderness School Board of Trustees, ms., 13 Nov. 1914, Holderness School Archives, New Hampshire.

123. Lorin Webster, minutes of the meeting of the Holderness School Board of Trustees, ms., 28 Sep. 1916, Holderness School Archives, New Hampshire.

124. Lorin Webster, minutes of the meeting of the Holderness School Board of Trustees, ms., 29 Oct. 1917, Holderness School Archives, New Hampshire.

Lorin Webster, minutes of the meeting of the Holderness School Board of Trustees, ms., 11 Jan. 1918, Holderness School Archives, New Hampshire.

125. Lorin Webster, minutes of the meeting of the Holderness School Board of Trustees, ms., 24 June 1918, Holderness School Archives, New Hampshire.

126. Webster 28 Sep. 1916.

    Webster 24 June 1918.

    Lorin Webster, minutes of the meeting of the Holderness School Board of Trustees, ms., 12 Dec. 1919, Holderness School Archives, New Hampshire.

127. Neal H. Barker, letter to Holderness School, 25 Jun. 1980.

128. Weld, Three-Quarter Mark 19.

129. "1908," Holderness Newsletter 2.4 (Dec. 1955): 4.

130. James C. Flanders, minutes of the meeting of the Holderness School Board of Trustees, ms., 14 Feb. 1922, Holderness School Archives, New Hampshire.

131. James C. Flanders, letter to Lorin Webster, 29 Jun. 1922, Holderness School Archives, New Hampshire.

132. "Improvements About the School," The Dial 2.1 (Nov. 1923): 5-6.

133. Niles 7.

134. Weld, Three-Quarter Mark 19.

135. Niles 7.

136. "Foreword," The Dial 4.1 (Dec. 1925): 2.

137. R. Richard Hill, "School Spirit," The Dial 3.3 (Jun. 1925): 5-6.

138. "News," The Dial 8.3 (Apr. 1930): 18-19.

139. Robert Eliot Marshall, "Foreword," The Dial 3.1 (Dec. 1924): 2-3.

140. Robert Eliot Marshall, minutes of the meeting of the Holderness School Board of Trustees, ms., 13 Oct. 1924, Holderness School Archives, New Hampshire.

141. "The New Colors," The Dial 2.2 (Jan. 1924): 11.

142. "Hockey," The Dial 5.1 (Mar. 1927): 15.

143. "Basketball," The Dial 4.4 (Dec. 1926): 12-13.

144. "Athletics," The Dial 4.2 (Apr. 1926): 17.

145. "School Notes," The Dial 2.3 (Apr. 1924): 13.

146. "Give Us a Hand," The Dial 1.5 (16 Apr. 1923): 2.

147. "The House Party," The Dial 2.3 (Apr. 1924): 14.

148. "The House Party" 14-15.

149. "Holderness News," The Dial 5.2 (May 1927): 19.

150. "School News," The Dial 5.4 (Nov. 1927): 16.

151. "Good Sportsmanship," The Dial 2.3 (Apr. 1924): 3.

152. Robert Eliot Marshall, minutes of the meeting of the Holderness School Board of Trustees, ms., 28 Sep. 1926, Holderness School Archives, New Hampshire.

153. Edward M. Parker, letter to Robert Eliot Marshall, 21 Jul. 1925, Holderness School Archives, New Hampshire.

154. Robert Eliot Marshall, letter to William S. Hubbard, 28 May 1928, Holderness School Archives, New Hampshire.

155. Niles 8.

156. "Editorial," The Dial 7.4 (Jun. 1929): 6.

157. Marshall 13 Oct. 1924.

158. Robert Eliot Marshall, minutes of the meeting of the Holderness School Board of Trustees, ms., 12 Oct. 1920, Holderness School Archives, New Hampshire.

159. Weld, Three-Quarter Mark 20.

160. Edgar B. Prescott, minutes of the meeting of the Holderness School Board of Trustees, ms., 30 Jan. 1930, Holderness School Archives, New Hampshire.

161. Prescott 30 Jan. 1930.

162. "News," The Dial 8.1 (Dec. 1929): 16-17.

163. [Edgar B. Prescott], minutes of the meeting of the Board of Trustees of Holderness School, ts., 30 Jan. 1930, Holderness School Archives, New Hampshire.

164. "The 50th Anniversary: Commencement Week," The Dial 8.4 (Jun. 1930): 39.

165. "The 50th Anniversary" 40.

166. Prescott 30 Jan. 1930.

167. "The New Holderness," The Dial 8.1 (Dec. 1929): 6.

168. "The New Holderness" 6.

169. Weld, Three-Quarter Mark 20.

170. Weld, Three-Quarter Mark 20.

171. "The Clubs," The Dial 9.1 (Dec. 1930): 6.

172. "News," The Dial 9.1 (Dec. 1930): 17.

173. "News," Dec. 1930 18.

174. "News," The Dial 9.2 (Feb. 1931): 36.

175. "News," Feb. 1931 37.

176. [Prescott] 30 Jan. 1930.

177. Weld, Three-Quarter Mark 20.

178. Brinton W. Woodward, Jr., speech, Newcomen Society Meeting, Holderness School, New Hampshire, 3 March 1979.

179. Weld, Three-Quarter Mark 21.

180. Weld, Three-Quarter Mark 21.

181. Weld, Three-Quarter Mark 22.

182. Niles 1-2.

183. Weld, Three-Quarter Mark 22-27.

184. Weld, Three-Quarter Mark 27.

185. Weld, Three-Quarter Mark 27.

186. Woodward, Newcomen Society speech.

187. Weld, Three-Quarter Mark 29.

188. Weld, Three-Quarter Mark 30.

189. Edric A. Weld, letter to alumni and friends of Holderness School, 15 Jul. 1940, Holderness School Archives, New Hampshire.

190. Edric A. Weld, "Letter to the Trustees," 23 Sep. 1940, Holderness School Archives, New Hampshire.

191. Weld, Three-Quarter Mark 40.

192. Edric A. Weld, "Bulletin to the Trustees," 25 Apr. 1941, Holderness School Archives, New Hampshire.

193. Edric A. Weld, "Report to the Trustees," 15 Feb. 1941, Holderness School Archives, New Hampshire.

194. Weld 25 Apr. 1941.

195. Edric A. Weld, In Time of War: For the Alumni of Holderness School (n.p.: n.p., [1943]).

196. Edric A. Weld, letter to the alumni, May 1945, Holderness School Archives, New Hampshire.

197. Weld May 1945.

198. Mary Anne Bodecker, letter to the author, 13 Oct. 2004.

199. Edric A. Weld, "Report of the Rector to the Trustees," 28 Sep. 1945, Holderness School Archives, New Hampshire.

200. Weld, Three-Quarter Mark 45.

201. Weld, Three-Quarter Mark 33.

202. "Holderness Students Take To the Slopes," The New Hampshire Churchman Mar. 1950 reprint: 1-2.

203. Weld 15 Feb. 1941.

204. Weld, Three-Quarter Mark 30, 40.

205. Weld, Three-Quarter Mark 40.

206. Weld, Three-Quarter Mark 30.

207. "Debating Club Into NFL Chapter," The Bull 3.7 (11 May 1949): 5.

208. "How Things Were," The Bull 14.2 (May 1970): 4.

209. Holderness School, Plymouth, New Hampshire [catalogue for the seventy-first year] (n.p.: n.p., [1949]) 7.

210. Holderness School Catalogue [1949] 7.

211. Edric A. Weld, "Report of the Rector: 1947," 11 Oct. 1947, Holderness School Archives, New Hampshire.

212. Edric A. Weld, "Annual Report of the Rector to the Trustees," 5 Oct. 1946, Holderness School Archives, New Hampshire.

213. Weld, Three-Quarter Mark 47.

214. [Edric A. Weld], "History and Present Requirements of the School," ts., Holderness School Archives, New Hampshire, [1951], 2.

215. Patricia S. Henderson, "The Final Lap," Holderness School 1879-1979: One Hundred Years (n.p.: n.p., [1979]) 65.

216. [Edric A. Weld], "Report to the Trustees," June 1951, Holderness School Archives, New Hampshire.

217. Weld, Three-Quarter Mark 47.

218. Lawrance W. Rathbun, minutes of the Development Committee of Holderness School, ts., 11 Mar. 1950, Holderness School Archives, New Hampshire.

219. [Donald C. Hagerman], report to the Trustees, [1955-1956], Holderness School Archives, New Hampshire.

220. [Hagerman] [1955-1956].

221. Woodward, Newcomen Society speech.

222. Woodward, Newcomen Society speech.

223. [Hagerman] [1955-1956].

224. Woodward, Newcomen Society speech.

225. [Hagerman] [1955-1956].

226. Henderson, "The Final Lap" 58.

227. Henderson, "The Final Lap" 58.

228. Henderson, "The Final Lap" 61.

229. Walter Deacon, "Traditional Rivals Clash as Undefeated Proctor Faces Holderness In Grid Finale," The Holderness Bull 15.2 (12 Nov. 1960): 1, 3.

230. "Proctor Academy Retains White Football In Thirty-Fifth Meeting of the Traditional Rivals," The Holderness Bull 16.2 (9 Dec. 1961): 1.

231. "Debators Win," The Bull 6.7 (6 Jun. 1962): 10.

232. "Annual Revival of Gilbert & Sullivan," The Bull 6.7 (6 Jun. 1962): 1.

233. Patricia S. Henderson, personal interview, 19 Oct. 2004.

234. Donald C. Hagerman, letter to alumni, parents, and friends of Holderness School, [1970], Holderness School Archives, New Hampshire.

235. "Faculty Notes," Holderness Newsletter 2.6 (Dec. 1957): 2.

236. "Activities," The Dial 1967: 82-84.

237. Herbert O. Waters, letter to Patricia S. Henderson, [1979].

238. Henderson, "The Final Lap" 78.

239. Woodward, Newcomen Society speech.

240. Edward Cayley, "The Hagermans Plan June Retirement," Holderness School Alumni News Fall 1976: 1-2.

241. Weld, Three-Quarter Mark 47.

242. Brinton W. Woodward, Jr., email to the author, 18 Oct. 2004.

243. Mayland H. Morse, Jr., letter to Holderness School alumni, parents, and friends, Feb. 1977, Holderness School Archives, New Hampshire.

244. James E. Brewer II, "Centennial Fund Achieves $3,500,000 Goal On Schedule," Holderness School Today 2.3 (Jul. 1979): 2.

245. W. Dexter Paine III, letter to Holderness School alumni, parents, and friends, [Feb. 2000], Holderness School Archives, New Hampshire.

246. Woodward 18 Oct. 2004.

247. Bart Nourse, "An Energy-Efficient House That Students Built," Center for Environmental Education Energy Newsletter 1.1 (Spring 1981): 2-3.

248. Nourse, "Energy-Efficient House" 2-3.

249. Brinton W. Woodward, Jr., letter to the Trustees, 17 Feb. 1978, Holderness School Archives, New Hampshire.

250. WM Design Group, Inc., "Master Plan Report: Present and Future Needs, Holderness School, Plymouth, New Hampshire," ts., 25 Feb. 1977, Holderness School Archives, New Hampshire, 3.

251. WM Design Group, Inc. 6.

252. Brinton W. Woodward, Jr., personal interview, 24 Oct. 2003.

253. Alfred C. Olivetti, minutes of the meeting of the Holderness School Board of Trustees, ms., 18 Nov. 1977, Holderness School Archives, New Hampshire.

254. Woodward 17 Feb. 1978.

255. Woodward 18 Oct. 2004.

256. John W. Boynton, "Admissions Report," ts., Holderness School Archives, New Hampshire, 12 Feb. 1978.

257. [Peter Barnum], "Admissions Planning: 1985-86," ts., Holderness School Archives, New Hampshire, [1985].

258. Woodward 18 Oct. 2004.

259. Enrollment report for Holderness School Admissions Office, ts., 12 Sep. 2001, Holderness School Archives, New Hampshire.

260. Woodward 24 Oct. 2003.

261. Woodward 24 Oct. 2003.

262. Woodward 17 Feb. 1978.

263. Woodward 24 Oct. 2003.

264. Woodward 17 Feb. 1978.

265. James E. Brewer II, "Service Committee Vitally Involved In Many Areas," Holderness School Today 4.1 (Jan. 1981): 7.

266. Don Hinman, "Habitat for Humanity," Holderness School Today 13.2 (Apr. 1990): 3-4.

267. Rick Carey, "Public Service Approved by Trustees and Faculty As Component of Diploma Requirements," Holderness School Today 15.3 (Sep. 1992): 3, 5.

268. Brinton W. Woodward, Jr., "Headmaster's Letter - Winter," Feb. 1985, Holderness School Archives, New Hampshire.

269. Brinton W. Woodward, Jr., letter to friends of Holderness School, Winter 1987, Holderness School Archives, New Hampshire.

270. James E. Brewer II, "Something In Comment," Holderness School Today 10.3 (Sep. 1987): 4.

271. "Holderness School: The Student Handbook, 1989-1990," [1989], Holderness School Archives, New Hampshire, 18.

272. Woodward 24 Oct. 2003.

273. Holderness School [catalogue for the one-hundred-seventeenth year] (n.p.: n.p., [1995?]) 30,36.

274. Woodward 24 Oct. 2003.

275. Paul Faber and Jim Brewer, "Stroudwood 'Rash Act' Entertaining Despite Over-Undertones," Holderness School Today 10.2 (Apr. 1987): 1, 5-6.

276. Brinton W. Woodward, Jr., letter to friends of Holderness School, Feb. 2000, Holderness School Archives, New Hampshire.

277. Paine [Feb. 2000].

278. Underwood 20.

279. Emily Wiggin Balch, letter to Augustus Wiggin, [c. 1877], Holderness School Archives, New Hampshire.

280. [Stetson].

281. "Baskets," The Argus 2.6 (Dec. 1902): 63.

282. "Baskets" 62.

283. "Editorial," The Argus 10.9 (June 1911): 160.

284. "Editorials," The Argus 5.5 (June 1905): 61-62.

285. "School Notes," The Argus 5.13 (Jun. 1906): 212.

286. "School Notes," The Argus 12.6 (May 1913): 122.
"Social Notes," The Argus 16.4 (May 1917): 7.

287. Holderness School, Plymouth, New Hampshire [catalogue for the fiftieth year] (n.p.: n.p., [1929]) 9.

288. Life At Holderness (n.p.: [Holderness School], [c. 1929]) [5].

289. "News," The Dial 10.1 (Dec. 1931): 28.

290. "News," Dec. 1931 26, 28.

291. "Having Learned of Each Other What Love Is," Holderness School Today, 17.3 (Fall 1998): 35.

292. Patricia S. Henderson, personal interview, Oct. 2003.

293. Henderson Oct. 2003.

294. Peter Rapelye, email to Holderness School Archives, 20 Oct. 2003.

295. "School Notes," The Argus 11.9 (June 1912): 188.

296. "Social Notes," The Argus 13.6-7 (Apr.-May 1914): 112.

297. "Editorials," The Argus 12.6 (May 1913): 112.

298. "Faculty," The Dial 1940: [14].

299. "News," Dec. 1931 25.

300. "The Fifty-Second Commencement," The Dial 10.4 (Jun. 1932): 9.

301. "Faculty," 1940 [14].

302. "Faculty," The Dial 1942: [13].

303. "Mrs. Salmon on Faculty of Holderness Central School," Holderness Newsletter 5.1 (Oct. 1956): 5.

304. Christopher K. Downs, Oral History Interview with Betsy Paine '80, ts., Holderness School Archives, New Hampshire, 21 Feb. 1990, 11.

305. Christopher K. Downs, Oral History Interview with Shelli Perkins, ts., Holderness School Archives, New Hampshire, 16 Mar. 1990, 7.

306. Balch [c. 1877].

307. "In Memoriam," The Bull 21.1 (Oct. 1966): 6.

308. Bertha Niles Hodgson, "Historical Outline 1886-1935," The Founding and Development of Saint Mary's School (n.p: n.p., [c.1950]) 7.

309. Hodgson 13-14.

310. Hodgson 18.

311. Christine Vaughan Moore, "The Moving," The Founding and Development of Saint Mary's School (n.p: n.p., [c.1950]) 30-31.

312. Henderson, "The Final Lap" 78.

313. James B. Godfrey, minutes of the meeting of the Holderness School Board of Trustees, ts., 17 Oct. 1969, Holderness School Archives, New Hampshire.

314. NAIS, "Evidence of the Trend Toward Mergers and Coeducation," mailing to independent schools, Jan. 1975.

315. NAIS Jan. 1975.

316. James B. Godfrey, minutes of the meeting of the Holderness School Board of Trustees, ts., 15 May 1970, Holderness School Archives, New Hampshire.

317. James B. Godfrey, minutes of the meeting of the Holderness School Board of Trustees, ts., 3 May 1971, Holderness School Archives, New Hampshire.

318. "Dorms," The Dial 1977: [n.p.].

319. Charles F. Leahy, letter to Mayland H. Morse, Jr., Esq., 25 Feb. 1970, Holderness School Archives, New Hampshire.

320. James B. Godfrey, minutes of the meeting of the Holderness School Board of Trustees, ts., 24 Apr. 1970, Holderness School Archives, New Hampshire.

321. Donald C. Hagerman, headmaster's newsletter, [Fall 1970], Holderness School Archives, New Hampshire.

322. Chris Graff, "Chapel Committee to Make Services a 'Relevant' Experience," The Bull 14.1 (Nov. 1969): 1-2.

323. James B. Godfrey, minutes of the meeting of the Holderness School Board of Trustees, ts., 13 Nov. 1970, Holderness School Archives, New Hampshire.

324. James B. Godfrey, minutes of the meeting of the Holderness School Board of Trustees, ts., 14 May 1971, Holderness School Archives, New Hampshire.

325. James B. Godfrey, minutes of the meeting of the Holderness School Board of Trustees, ts., 28 Jan. 1972, Holderness School Archives, New Hampshire.

326. A.D. Ayrault, letter to the Education Committee of the Lakeside School Board of Trustees, 7 Jan. 1970, Holderness School Archives, New Hampshire.

327. Janice Ruell, "A Day Girl Looks At Holderness," Holderness School Alumni News Spring 1975: 4.

328. Downs, Interview with Shelli Perkins 2.

329. Henderson, "The Final Lap" 62.

330. Downs, Interview with Shelli Perkins 1-2.

331. Ruell 4.

332. Ruell 4.

333. Downs, Interview with Shelli Perkins 12.

334. Christopher K. Downs, Oral History Interview with Patricia Henderson, ts., Holderness School Archives, New Hampshire, 10 Apr. 1990, 2.

335. Douglas N. Everett, minutes of the meeting of the Holderness School Board of Trustees, ts., 14 May 1976, Holderness School Archives, New Hampshire.

336. Thomas Armstrong, notes on coeducation study meetings, ts., Aug. 1976, Holderness School Archives, New Hampshire.

337. Alfred C. Olivetti, minutes of the meeting of the Holderness School Board of Trustees, ms., 14 Oct. 1977, Holderness School Archives, New Hampshire.

338. Brinton W. Woodward, Jr., "Statement for Coeducation at Holderness," Nov. 1977, Holderness School Archives, New Hampshire.

339. Alfred C. Olivetti, minutes of the meeting of the Holderness School Board of Trustees, ts., 18 Nov. 1977, Holderness School Archives, New Hampshire.

340. Jay Stroud, letter to Trustees of Holderness School, Feb. 1978, Holderness School Archives, New Hampshire.

341. Woodward 24 Oct. 2003.

342. Henderson, "The Final Lap" 62-63, 78, 82.

343. Henderson, "The Final Lap" 80.

344. George Hodges, In the Beauty of Holderness (Boston: Church Militant Press, 1903) 9, 15.

345. George Hodges, Holderness–An Account of the Beginnings of a New Hampshire Town (Cambridge: The Riverside Press, 1907) 40.

346. Hodges, Beginnings 71, 69.

347. Howe and Keith 7.

348. Hodges, Beginnings 69.

349. Hodges, <u>Beauty of Holderness</u> 18.

350. Sargent [2].

351. H. Hill 15.

352. Niles 4.

353. H. Hill 15.

354. "Holderness Head and Faculty," <u>The Argus</u> 16.5 (June 1917): 4.

355. "Personals" 100.

356. "School Notes," <u>The Volunteer</u> 2.3 (Dec. 1888): 9.

357. "Society Notes," <u>The Argus</u> 2.4 (Oct. 1902): 39.

358. "School Notes," Jun. 1906 212.

359. "School Notes," <u>The Argus</u> 4.5 (Jun. 1904): 331.

360. "News of the School," <u>Holderness News</u> 3.4 (May 1955): 3.

361. "Statement of Offerings: Chapel of the Holy Cross, Holderness School," <u>The Dial</u> 4.4 (Dec. 1926): 15.

362. Edric A. Weld, "Report to the Trustees," [June] 1944, Holderness School Archives, New Hampshire.

363. <u>Holderness News-Letter</u> 1.6 (July 1953): 1.

364. James B. Godfrey, minutes of the meeting of the Holderness School Executive Board of Trustees, ms., 7 Aug. 1969, Holderness School Archives, New Hampshire.

365. "School Notes," Apr. 1924 13.

366. "School Notes," Apr. 1889 4.

367. "St. Barnabas's Church, Berlin, N.H.," <u>The Dial</u> 4.4 (Dec. 1926): 14.

368. "News of the School," <u>Holderness News</u> 5.3 (Mar. 1957): 2.

369. "News of the School," Mar. 1957 2.

370. Underwood 14.

371. Edric A. Weld, "Holderness School," <u>The New Hampshire Churchman</u> Feb. 1950 reprint: 1.

372. "Freedom of Worship?" <u>The Bull</u> 4.4 (8 Feb. 1950): 1-2.

373. Edric A. Weld, "The Four Freedoms," [1950], Holderness School Archives, New Hampshire.

374. Joanna Snyder, "Chapel," Holderness School Alumni News Fall 1975: 13.

375. J. Ritzman, "Mr. Norman," The Bull 14.1(10 Nov. 1959): 4.

376. Donald C. Hagerman, Chapel sermon, ts., [c. 1968], Holderness School Archives, New Hampshire, 2.

377. Hyde Post, "Bishop Hall Holds Forum," The Bull 13.3 (Mar. 1969): 2.

378. Donald C. Hagerman, "Holderness Faces the 1970's," [1971], Holderness School Archives, New Hampshire.

379. Donald C. Hagerman, headmaster's newsletter, [1971], Holderness School Archives, New Hampshire, 2.

380. Snyder, "Chapel" 13.

381. Brinton W. Woodward, Jr., letter to Trustees, 17 Feb. 1978, Holderness School Archives, New Hampshire.

382. Walt Kesler, "Faculty Members Speak at Thursday Evening Chapel During the Winter Term" Holderness School Today 4.2 (Apr. 1981): 2.

383. Brinton W. Woodward, Jr., "From the Schoolhouse," Holderness School Today 19.1 (2000): [inside front cover].

384. "The Early Days of Holderness," Ollapodrida '90 1 (1890): 22.

385. "News," Feb. 1931 36.

386. Edric A. Weld, "The Rector's Message," The Dial 10.1 (Dec. 1931): 8.

387. "School Notes," The Volunteer 2.7 (May 1889): 4.

388. "School Notes," Jun. 1904 331.

    "The Brewster Trip," The Argus 4.6 (Oct. 1904): 361.

389. "Holderness News," May 1927 19.

390. "News," The Dial 8.4 (June 1930): 25.

391. Allen Early, "Holderness Fire Department," The Bull 2.1 (24 Oct. 1947): 3.

392. "School News," Nov. 1927 16.

393. Weld 15 Feb. 1941.

394. [Holderness School Newsletter] 3 Dec. 1959: 1.

395. Jim Ricker, "Vestry Plans Hospital Trips; Discusses Charity Plans," The Bull 17.3 (15 Mar. 1963): 2.

"Service Committee Vitally Involved In Many Areas," Holderness School Today 4.1 (Jan. 1981): 7.

396. Weld, Three-Quarter Mark 22-27.

397. Weld, Three-Quarter Mark 27.

398. Carey, "Public Service" 3.

399. Carey, "Public Service" 3.

400. "Holderness School," The Argus 2.3 (May 1902): 27.

401. "School Notes," Apr. 1889 5.

402. Holderness News-Letter 1.3 (Feb. 1953): 1.

403. Joanna Snyder, "Swedish Custom Becomes Holderness Tradition," Holderness School Alumni News Spring 1975: 12.

404. Brinton W. Woodward, Jr., headmaster's newsletter, Winter 1990, Holderness School Archives, New Hampshire.

405. [Stetson].

406. Holderness School 1883 2.

407. Catalogue of the Holderness School for Boys, Plymouth, New Hampshire: Seventh Year, 1885 (n.p.: n.p., [1885]) 5.

408. Catalogue of Holderness School for Boys, Plymouth, N.H.: Thirteenth Year, 1891–'92 (Concord, New Hampshire: Republican Press Association, 1892) 6.

409. Catalogue of Holderness School for Boys, Plymouth, N.H.: Fourteenth Year, 1892–93 (Plymouth, New Hampshire: The Record Publishing Company, 1893) 8-10.

410. Holderness School Catalogue 1893 8.

411. Holderness School Catalogue 1893 8.

412. Holderness School Catalogue 1892 6.

413. Holderness School Catalogue 1893 8.

414. Catalogue of Holderness School for Boys, Plymouth, N.H.: Twenty-Third Year, 1901–1902 (Concord, New Hampshire: The Rumford Press, 1902) 13-15.

415. Catalogue of Holderness School for Boys, Plymouth, New Hampshire: Thirtieth Year, 1908-1909 (Concord, New Hampshire: Rumford Printing Company, 1909) 14.

416. Catalogue of Holderness School for Boys, Plymouth, New Hampshire: Thirty-First Year, 1909-1910 (Concord, New Hampshire: The Rumford Press, 1910) 15.

417. Catalogue of Holderness School for Boys, Plymouth, New Hampshire: Thirty-Second Year, 1910-1911 (Concord, New Hampshire: The Rumford Press, 1911) 16.

418. Catalogue of Holderness School for Boys, Plymouth, New Hampshire: Thirty-Fifth Year 1913-1914 (Andover, Massachusetts: The Andover Press, 1915) 13.

419. Catalogue of Holderness School for Boys, Plymouth, New Hampshire: Thirty-Eighth Year 1916-1917 (Manchester, New Hampshire: Williams Printing Company, 1917) 13.

420. Catalogue of Holderness School for Boys, Plymouth, New Hampshire: Thirty-Ninth Year 1917-1918 (Manchester, New Hampshire: Williams Printing Company, 1918) 13.

421. Catalogue of Holderness School for Boys, Plymouth, New Hampshire: Forty-First Year 1919-1920 (Plymouth, New Hampshire: n.p., 1920) 14.

422. Catalogue of Holderness School for Boys, Plymouth, New Hampshire: Forty-Third Year 1922–1923 (Plymouth, New Hampshire: n.p., 1922) 14.

423. Holderness School for Boys, Plymouth, New Hampshire: 'Pro Deo et Genere Humano' Forty-Ninth Year 1927-1928 (Manchester, New Hampshire: Lew A. Cummings Co., [1928]) 17.

424. Holderness School Catalogue [1929] 19-22.

425. Holderness School Catalogue [1929] 22.

426. Holderness School [catalogue for the fifty-third year] (n.p.: n.p., [1932]) [13].

427. Holderness School Founded 1879, Plymouth, New Hampshire [catalogue for the sixty-eighth year] (n.p.: n.p., [1947?]) 6.

428. Holderness School Catalogue [1947?] 16-19.

429. Holderness School Catalogue [1947?] 13.

430. Holderness School Catalogue and Course Guide 1976-77 (n.p.: n.p., [1976]) 16, 19.

431. Holderness School Faculty and Course Guide 1983-1984 (n.p.: n.p., [1983]) [6-13].

432. [Rick Carey], "This Way to the Top," in Holderness School Today 16.3 (1997): 9.

433. [Carey], "This Way to the Top" 9.

434. "School Widens Its Horizons In Regard To College Admissions," The Bull 15.1 (29 Oct. 1960): 1.

435. Walt Kesler, "First College Night," Holderness School Today 8.1 (1985): 1-3.

436. Kesler, "College Night" 3.

437. "Office of College Counseling," Holderness School Website, Holderness School, 21 Sep. 2004 <http://www.holderness.org/students/college.asp>.

438. "Editorials," The Argus 16.4 (May 1917): 2.

439. A.M. Dunstan, "Address to the Boys of the School," The Argus 16.3 (Mar. 1917): 4.

440. Holderness School Catalogue 1918 13.

441. "Editorials," May 1917 2.

442. Holderness School Founded 1879, Plymouth, New Hampshire [catalogue for the sixty-fifth year] (n.p.: n.p., [1943?]) 9.

443. Edric Weld, "Annual Report of the Rector to the Trustees," 10 Oct. 1942, Holderness School Archives, New Hampshire, 1.

444. Weld, 10 Oct. 1942 4.

445. Weld, 10 Oct. 1942 4.

446. Holderness School Founded 1879, Plymouth, New Hampshire [catalogue for the seventieth year] (n.p.: n.p., [1948?]) 5.

447. Henderson, "The Final Lap" 58.

448. Henderson, "The Final Lap" 58.

449. Roger Glazebrook, "Projects in Special Fields Conducted By Juniors and Seniors," The Bull 16.4 (9 June 1962): 3.

450. Holderness School Catalogue [1976] 20.

451. Donald C. Hagerman, newsletter to alumni, parents and friends, [1970], Holderness School Archives, New Hampshire.

452. Jim Brewer, "Senior Projects Offer Variety," Holderness School Alumni News Fall 1977: 8-9.

453. Hagerman "Holderness Faces the 1970's."

454. "Out Back," Holderness School Website, Holderness School, 20 Sep. 2004 <http://www.holderness.org/programs/out_back.asp>.

455. "Trip Into the Wilderness Gives Class Time to Reflect," unidentified newspaper clipping, [3 Mar. 1974], Holderness School Archives, New Hampshire.

456. [Fred Beams], "Holderness Outward Bound," [1969], Holderness School Archives, New Hampshire, 1, 2, 6.

457. Joanna Snyder, "Wallace Challenge Met," Holderness School Alumni News Spring 1976: 9.

458. Joanna Snyder, "Outward Bound 1976," Holderness School Alumni News Spring 1976: 16-17.

459. Robert S. MacArthur, "Report on the Holderness School Out Back Program," 1980, Holderness School Archives, New Hampshire, 1, 3, 4, 5-6.

460. James E. Brewer II, "Something in Comment," Holderness School Today 4.2 (Apr. 1981): 2.

461. Brewer, "Something in Comment" Apr. 1981 2.

462. Richard Adams Carey, "Wilderness for the Soul: Artward Bound at the Holderness School," Independent School Winter 1997: 13-14.

463. Brewer, "Something in Comment" Apr. 1981 2.

464. Brewer, "Something in Comment" Apr. 1981 2.

465. "Roots of Our Time: Colloquium Does 'Twenties,' First Step in Five Year Series," Holderness School Today 8.3 (Apr. 1985): 1.

466. Hinman 4-5.

467. "Holderness Habitat 1999 Permission Form," 1999, Holderness School Archives, New Hampshire.

468. Editorial, June 1888 1.

469. Editorial, Volunteer 2.1 1.

470. Editorial, The Volunteer 2.6 (Apr. 1889): 2.

471. "School Notes," May 1889 6.

472. "Editorials," The Argus 6.5 (Mar. 1907): 59.

473. "Athletic Notes," The Argus 4.1 (Feb. 1904): 236.

474. "Cross Country," The Dial 2.1 (Nov. 1923): 21.

475. "Ice Hockey," The Dial 7.4 (June 1929): 25.

476. "Tennis," The Dial 4.3 (May-June 1926): 23.

477. "The Track Revival," The Dial 2.4 (June 1924): 23.

478. "Golf," The Dial 10.4 (June 1932): 26.

479. "Skiing," The Dial 14.2 (Mar. 1936): 27.

480. "Soccer," The Dial 1953: [76].

481. "Wrestling," The Dial 1970: 58.

482. "Sailing Club," The Dial Spring Supplement 1973: 117.

483. "Rock Climbing," The Dial 1970: 65.

484. "Lacrosse," The Dial 1961: 78.

485. "Girls Field Hockey," The Dial 1980: 50.

486. Franz Nicolay, "Spring Sports," Holderness School Today 14.3 (1995): 9.

487. Holderness School: An Episcopal School for Boys in the Foothills of the White Mountains [catalogue for the fifty-first year] (Manchester, New Hampshire: Lew A. Cummings Co., [1929]) 12.

488. Holderness School Founded 1879, Plymouth, New Hampshire [catalogue for the fifty-fifth year] (n.p.: n.p., [1933?]) 4.

489. Henderson, "The Final Lap" 60.

490. Holderness School Founded 1879, Plymouth, New Hampshire [catalogue for the fifty-eighth year] (n.p.: n.p., [1936?]) 11.

491. Holderness School Founded 1879, Plymouth, New Hampshire [catalogue for the sixtieth year] (n.p.: n.p., [1938?]) 3, 8.

"Faculty," 1940 [13].

"Faculty," 1942 [11].

492. "Faculty," The Dial 1946: [11].

493. "Faculty," The Dial 1952: [10, 12].

494. "Highlights of Holderness School Ski Record," [1974], Holderness School Archives, New Hampshire.

495. "To the Mountaintop: Holderness Celebrates the Winter Olympics," ts., 2002, Holderness School Archives, New Hampshire, 6.

496. Henderson, "The Final Lap" 61.

497. Don Henderson, "A Quarter Century of Holderness Skiing," Holderness School Alumni News Spring 1976: 1-2.

498. "Faculty," The Dial 1961: 13.

499. Henderson, "The Final Lap" 61.

500. Steve Gaskill, "Ski Jumping," Holderness School Today 10.2 (Apr. 1987): 9.

501. Paul Elkins, "Snowboarding," Holderness School Today 14.2 (May 1991): 9.

502. Daniel Pearl, "Varsity Freestyle Ski," Holderness School Today 17.32 (Spring 1998): 15.

503. Georg Capaul, personal interview, Spring 2004.

504. [Stetson].

505. Underwood 68, 83.

506. Underwood 74.

507. Underwood 20.

508. "School Notes," The Argus 7.1 (Oct. 1907): 12.

509. "School News," Nov. 1927 15.

510. [Stetson].

511. "Prize Essay: The Elements of Camp Life at Holderness School," Ollapo-drida '91 2 (1891): 23.

512. "Elements of Camp Life" 24.

513. "Elements of Camp Life" 24.

514. Underwood 24.

515. Chocurua Island Chapel, 27 Sep. 2004 <http://www.churchisland.org>.

516. Underwood 97.

517. "Elements of Camp Life" 25.

518. "Editorials," The Argus 3.6 (Oct. 1903): 162.

519. "School Notes," The Argus 4.7 (Nov. 1904): 386.

520. Holderness School Outing Club, "Outing Club Log Book #1," ms., [1974], Holderness School Archives, New Hampshire, 116-117.

521. James E. Brewer II, "Helen and Scott Nearing Keynote Speakers in Centennial Colloquium," Holderness School Today 2.2 (Apr. 1979): 1.

522. Bartley B. Nourse, Jr., "Doom, Gloom, Optimism Are Ingredients of the April 20 Centennial Colloquium," Holderness School Today 2.3 (Jul. 1979): 1, 8.

523. Brewer, "Helen and Scott Nearing" 1.

524. Bartley B. Nourse, Jr., "Bioshelter Construction Moves Toward Fall Completion," Holderness School Today 2.2 (Apr. 1979): 7.

525. Nourse, "Bioshelter Construction" 7.

526. James E. Brewer II, "Project Reports From 52 Seniors Emphasize Variety, Involvement, and Creativity," Holderness School Today 2.3 (Jul. 1979): 8.

527. James E. Brewer II, "Something In Comment," Holderness School Today 10.1 (Sep. 1986): 2.

528. Rebecca M. Stratton, "Projects '90 Far-Flung Innovative Learning Experiences," Holderness School Today 13.3 (Sep. 1990): 3.

529. Mattie Ford, "Milfoil Extraction: Senior Project," ts., 1 Jun. 2004, Barbara Lawrence Alfond Library, New Hampshire.

530. Bartley B. Nourse, Jr., "Two Energy Committees Function to Conserve," Holderness School Today 4.1 (Jan. 1981): 2.

531. "Recycle-Bulls," Holderness School Website, Holderness School, 9/27/ 2004 <http://www.holderness.org/students/recycle.asp>.

532. Underwood 53.

533. Holderness School Ocarina Quartette, [1889], Holderness School Photo Archives, New Hampshire.

534. "Musical Organizations," Ollapodrida '90 1 (1890): 62.

535. "Fitch, Clyde." Encyclopædia Britannica. 2004. Encyclopædia Britannica Online. 12 Oct. 2004 <http://search.eb.com/eb/article?tocId=9034415>.

536. Hubbard 14.

537. Underwood 37.

538. "Literary Organizations," Ollapodrida '90 1 (1890): 58.

539. "Camps," Ollapodrida '90 1 (1890): 34-40.

540. "Secret Societies in order of their Establishment," Ollapodrida '90 1 (1890): 26-32.

541. "Literary Organizations" 56.

"Miscellaneous," Ollapodrida '90 1 (1890): 64-65.

542. "School Notes," Apr. 1889 6.

543. "Programme: Holderness School The Evening of Closing Day," ts., 11 June 1902, Holderness School Archives, New Hampshire.

544. Twenty-Fifth Anniversary Reunion, [1905], Holderness School Photo Archives, New Hampshire.

545. Holderness School Catalogue 1932 [12-13].

546. Holderness School Catalogue 1932 [5-6].

547. Holderness School Founded 1879, Plymouth, New Hampshire [catalogue for the fifty-fifth year] (n.p.: n.p., [1934]) [15-18].

548. Weld, Three-Quarter Mark 30-33.

549. "News," The Dial 10.2 (Mar. 1932): 19.

550. "Mr. Pitt Parker," The Bull 16 Mar. 1943: 8.

551. "News," The Dial 10.3 (May 1932): 13.

552. "The Great La Follette," The Bull Jan. 1944: 2.

553. Weld 15 Feb. 1941.

554. "Dartmouth Concert," The Bull 2.4 (30 Jan. 1948): 5.

555. Holderness School Catalogue [1934] [15-18].

556. "Faculty," The Dial 1947: [7-14].

557. Herbert O. Waters, "Herbert Waters, N.A.," ts., [c. 1983], Holderness School Archives, New Hampshire.

558. Herbert O. Waters, "Memorandum for the Rector," 13 Mar. 1947, Holderness School Archives, New Hampshire.

559. "Faculty," The Dial 1963: 10.

   Donald C. Hagerman, letter to Herbert O. Waters, 16 Apr. 1977, Holderness School Archives, New Hampshire.

560. Holderness School Catalogue [1976] [8-9].

561. David Lockwood, personal interview, 7 Oct. 2004.

562. Herbert O. Waters, letter to Donald C. Hagerman, 11 Mar. 1965, Holderness School Archives, New Hampshire.

563. Herbert O. Waters, letter to Donald C. Hagerman, [c. 1954], Holderness School Archives, New Hampshire.

564. "Scholarships and Endowments," Holderness School Website, Holderness School, 12 Oct. 2004 <http://www.holderness.org/alumni/a_schol.asp>.

565. A. Dewart, "New Dorm To Be Occupied In January," The Bull 14.1 (10 Nov. 1959): 1.

566. "The Carpenter Arts Center," Holderness School Today 21.2 (Fall 2002): 5.

567. "The Carpenter Arts Center" 4.

568. "The Carpenter Arts Center" 5.

569. "The Carpenter Arts Center" 5.

570. Lockwood, 7 Oct. 2004.

571. "Food Delivery," <u>Holderness School Website</u>, Holderness School, 8 Dec. 2003 <http://www.holderness.org/features/feature.asp?ID=74>.

572. Chris Mumford, "Memorial Scholarship Fund Moving Ahead," <u>Holderness School Website</u>, Holderness School, 5 Feb. 2003 <http://www.holderness.org/article.asp?ID=116>.

573. "Holderness School Strategic Plan," May 2003, Holderness School Archives, New Hampshire, 1.

574. "Holderness School Strategic Plan" 2.

575. Stephen D. Solberg, "Technology Conference Planned for Faculty," <u>Holdernet News</u> 2.3 (25 Apr. 2003): 1.

576. "Holderness School Strategic Plan" 2.

577. "Holderness School Strategic Plan" 3.

578. "Faculty," <u>The Dial</u> 1978: 8-18.

579. "Faculty," <u>The Dial</u> 2001: 40-47.

580. "Trustees," <u>Faces 2004-2005</u> 2004: 17.

581. Rick Carey, "Piper Orton '74 Elected Board Chair," <u>Holderness School Website</u>, Holderness School, 21 Oct. 2004 <http://www.holderness.org/article.asp?ID=305>.

582. "Holderness School Strategic Plan" 3.

583. "Holderness School Strategic Plan" 3.

584. "Diversity at Holderness," <u>Holderness School Website</u>, Holderness School, 19 Oct. 2004 <http://www.holderness.org/students/diversity.asp?node1=1&togglenode=node2>.

585. "Holderness School Strategic Plan" 3.

586. "2003 Livermore Renovations," <u>Holderness School Website</u>, Holderness School, 19 Oct. 2004 <http://www.holderness.org/features/2003_livermore/index.asp>.

587. Stephen D. Solberg, "Wireless Project Wraps Up," <u>Holdernet News</u> 3.3 (2 Jul. 2004): 2.

588. Stephen D. Solberg, "Filtered Internet: Coming to a Dorm Room Near You," <u>Holdernet News</u> 3.3 (2 Jul. 2004): 4.

589. Peter Hendel, email to Holderness School faculty, 28 Sep. 2004.

590. "Holderness School Strategic Plan" 4.

591. "Holderness School Strategic Plan" 4.